S0-AZB-984

The Mind Parasites

Colin Wilson has also written

THE OUTSIDER

RELIGION AND THE REBEL

THE AGE OF DEFEAT

THE STRENGTH TO DREAM

ORIGINS OF THE SEXUAL IMPULSE

BEYOND THE OUTSIDER

INTRODUCTION TO THE NEW EXISTENTIALISM

RASPUTIN AND THE FALL OF THE ROMANOVS

AN ENCYCLOPEDIA OF MURDER (with Pat Pitman)

EAGLE AND EARWIG (Essays on Books and Authors)

CHORDS AND DISCORDS (Essays on Music)

SEX AND THE INTELLIGENT TEENAGER

VOYAGE TO A BEGINNING (Autobiography)

THE OCCULT

and these novels—

RITUAL IN THE DARK

ADRIFT IN SOHO

THE WORLD OF VIOLENCE

NECESSARY DOUBT

THE GLASS CAGE

THE SEX DIARY OF GERARD SORME

THE BLACK ROOM

THE PHILOSOPHER'S STONE

The Mind Parasites

Colin Wilson

ONEIRIC PRESS / WINGBOW PRESS
Berkeley, California

Copyright © 1967 by Colin Wilson. All rights reserved. Printed in the United States of America.

No part of this book may be reproduced in any manner whatsoever without the written permission of the publisher except in the case of brief quotations embodied in critical articles and reviews.

Published by Oneiric Press.
Distributed by Bookpeople, 2929 Fifth Street, Berkeley, California 94710.

Cover image by Karl Mills, copyright 1977 by Scientific Photo Arts.

ISBN 0–914728–27–X.

Thirteenth printing: September 1990

for August Derleth
who suggested it

I *must*, before I die, find *some* way to say the essential thing that is in me, that I have never said yet – a thing that is not love or hate or pity or scorn, but the very breath of life, fierce and coming from far away, bringing into human life the vastness and the fearful passionless force of non-human things . . .

BERTRAND RUSSELL
Letter to Constance Malleson, 1918,
quoted in
My Philosophical Development p. 261

PREFATORY NOTE

We make no apology for devoting Volume III of the *Cambridge History of the Nuclear Age* to this new edition of that important document known as *The Mind Parasites* by Professor Gilbert Austin.

The Mind Parasites is, of course, a composite document made up from various papers, tape recordings, and verbatim reports of conversations with Professor Austin. The first edition, which was only about half the size of the present one, was published shortly after Professor Austin's disappearance in 2007, and before the *Pallas* had been found by Captain Ramsay's expedition. It consisted mainly of the notes made at the request of Colonel Spencer, and of the tape recording numbered 12xm, in the library of London University. The later edition that appeared in 2012 included the transcript of the shorthand conversation taken down by Leslie Purvison on 14 January, 2004. Inserted into these transcripts was material from two articles written by Austin for the *Historical Review*, and from his preface to Karel Weissman's *Historical Reflections*.

This new edition retains the old text *in toto*, and includes completely new material from the so-called Martinus File, that was for many years in the possession of Mrs Sylvia Austin, and that is now in the World Historical Archive. The editors have made clear in the footnotes* the sources from which various sections have been drawn, and have

---

* Mostly omitted from this popular edition.

utilized the still unpublished Autobiographical Notes written by Austin in 2001.

No edition of the *Mind Parasites* can claim to be definitive. It has been our aim to arrange the material in such a way that it forms a continual narrative. Where it was thought to be strictly relevant, material from Austin's philosophical papers has been added, and one short passage from the introduction to *Homage to Edmund Husserl*, edited by Austin and Reich. The resulting narrative seems, in the opinion of the editors, to support the views they advanced in *New Light on the Pallas Mystery*. But it should be emphasized that this was not their aim. They have tried to include all relevant material, and believe that the justice of this claim will be demonstrated when Northwestern University completes its edition of the *Complete Papers of Gilbert Austin*.

H.S.   W.P.

St Henry's College, Cambridge,
2014

(This section is transcribed from a tape recording made by Dr Austin a few months before his disappearance. It has been edited by H. F. Spencer.*)

A story as complex as this has no obvious starting point; neither am I able to follow Colonel Spencer's suggestion of ' beginning at the beginning and going on to the end ', since history has a habit of meandering. The best plan is probably to tell my personal story of the battle against the mind parasites, and to leave the rest of the picture to the historians.

My own story, then, begins on the 20th of December 1994, when I returned home from a meeting of the Middlesex Archaeological Society, before whom I had delivered a lecture on the ancient civilizations of Asia Minor. It had been a most lively and stimulating evening; there is no pleasure more satisfying than discoursing on a subject that is close to your heart in front of a completely attentive audience. Add to this that our dinner had finished with an excellent claret of the 1980's, and it will be understood that I was in a most cheerful and agreeable frame of mind when I inserted my key in the front door of my flat in Covent Garden.

My telescreen was ringing as I came in, but it stopped before I reached it. I glanced into the recording slot; it registered a Hampstead number that I recognized as that of Karel Weissman. It was a quarter to twelve, and I was sleepy; I decided to ring him back in the morning. But somehow, I felt uncomfortable as I undressed for bed. We were very old friends, and he frequently rang me up late

*Colonel H. F. Spencer, Head of the World Historical Archive, in which all Dr Austin's papers are preserved.

at night to ask me to look something up in the British Museum (where I spent most mornings). Yet this time, some faint psychic alarm bell made me uncomfortable; I went to the screen in my dressing-gown and dialled his number. It rang for a long time; I was about to hang up when the face of his secretary appeared on the screen. He said: 'You have heard the news?' 'What news?' I asked. 'Dr Weissman is dead.' I was so stunned that I had to sit down. I finally mustered the wit to ask: 'How should I have known?' 'It is in the evening papers.' I told him I had only just come in. He said: 'Ah, I see. I've been trying to ring you all evening. Could you possibly come up here right away?'

'But why? Is there anything I can do? Is Mrs Weissman well?'

'She is in a state of shock.'

'But how did he die?'

Baumgart said, without changing his expression: 'He committed suicide.'

I remember staring at him blankly for several seconds, then shouting:

'What the devil are you talking about? That's impossible.'

'There can be no possible doubt. Please come here as soon as you can.'

He started to remove the plug; I screamed:

'Do you want to drive me mad? Tell me what happened!'

'He took poison. There is almost nothing else I can tell you. But his letter says we should contact you immediately. So please come. We are all very tired.'

I called a helicab, and then dressed in a state of mental numbness, telling myself that this was impossible. I had known Karel Weissman for thirty years, ever since we were students at Uppsala. He was in every way a remarkable man: brilliant, perceptive, patient, and of immense drive and energy. *It was impossible.* Such a man could never commit suicide. Oh, I was fully aware that the world suicide

10

rate had multiplied by fifty since the mid-century, and that sometimes the most unexpected people kill themselves. But to tell me that Karel Weissman had committed suicide was like telling me that one and one made three. He had not an atom of self-destruction in his composition. In every way, he was one of the least neurotic, best integrated men I had ever known.

Could it, I wondered, have been murder? Had he, perhaps, been assassinated by an agent of the Central Asiatic Powers? I had heard of stranger things; political assassination had become an exact science in the second part of the eighties, and the deaths of Hammelmann and Fuller had taught us that even a scientist working under high security conditions is not safe. But Karel was a psychologist, and he had, as far as I knew, no connection of any kind with the government. His main income came from a large industrial corporation, who paid him to devise ways of combating dyno-neuroses and generally increasing productivity.

Baumgart was waiting for me when the taxi landed on the roof. The moment we were alone, I asked him: 'Could it be murder?' He replied: 'It is not impossible, of course, but there is no reason to think so. He retired to his room at three this afternoon to write a paper, telling me that he was not to be disturbed. His window was locked, and I was sitting at a desk in the anteroom during the next two hours. At five, his wife brought tea, and found him dead. He left a letter in his own handwriting, and had washed down the poison with a glass of water from the toilet.'

Half an hour later, I was convinced that my friend had indeed committed suicide. The only alternative was that Baumgart had killed him; yet I could not believe this. Baumgart had the control and impassiveness of a Swiss, but I could tell that he was deeply shaken, and on the point of an emotional breakdown; no man is a good enough actor to simulate these things. Besides, there was the letter in Karel's handwriting. Since Pomeroy produced the electro-comparison machine, forgery had become the rarest of crimes.

I left that house of gloom at two in the morning, having spoken to no one but Baumgart. I had not seen my dead friend, and neither did I want to, for I am told that the face of one who dies from cyanide is horrible. The tablets he had used had been taken from a psycho-neurotic patient only that morning.

The letter in itself was strange. It offered no word of regret for the act of self-destruction. The handwriting was shaky, but the wording was precise. It stated which of his possessions was to be left to his son, and which to his wife. It asked that I should be called as soon as possible to take charge of his scientific papers, and mentioned a sum of money that was to be paid to me, and a further sum that was to be used, if necessary, in their publication. I saw a photostat of the letter – the police had taken the original – and I knew that it was almost certainly genuine. Electronic analysis confirmed my view the following morning.

Yes, a most strange letter. Three pages long, and written with apparent calm. But why had he suggested that I should be contacted *immediately*? Could it be that his papers contained the clue? Baumgart had already considered the possibility, and had spent the evening examining them. He had found nothing there to justify Karel's demand for haste. A large proportion of the papers concerned the Anglo-Indian Computers Corporation, his employer; these would naturally be made available to the firm's other research officers. The remainder were various papers on existential psychology, Maslovian transactionism and the rest. An almost completed book dealt with the uses of psychedelic drugs.

Now, in the last named work, it seemed to me that I had found a clue. When Karel and I were at Uppsala, we spent a great deal of time discussing problems of the meaning of death, the limits of human consciousness, and so on. I was

12

writing a thesis on the Egyptian Book of the Dead, whose actual title, Ru nu pert em hru, means ' the book of coming forth by day '. I was concerned only with the symbolism of this ' dark night of the soul ', of the perils encountered by the disembodied spirit on its night-long journey to Amentet. But Karel had insisted that I should study the Tibetan Book of the Dead – an entirely different cup of tea – and compare the two. Now, as any student of these works knows, the Tibetan book is a Buddhist document whose religious background bears no resemblance whatever to that of the ancient Egyptians. I felt that to compare the two would be a waste of time, a mere exercise in pedantry. However, Karel succeeded in stimulating in me a certain interest in the Tibetan book for its own sake, with the consequence that we spent many a long evening discussing it. Psychedelic drugs were at the time almost unobtainable, since Aldous Huxley's book on mescalin had made them fashionable among addicts. However, we discovered an article by René Daumal describing how he had once made similar experiments with ether. Daumal had soaked a handkerchief in ether, which he then held to his nose. When he lost consciousness, his hand dropped, and he would quickly recover. Daumal attempted to describe his visions under ether, and they impressed and excited us. His main point was the same as that made by so many mystics: that although he was ' unconscious ' under ether, he had a sense that what he experienced was far *realler* than his everyday experience of the world. Now, both Karel and I agreed on one thing – no matter how dissimilar our temperaments might be in others – that our everyday lives had a quality of *unreality*. We could so well understand Chuang Tzu, who said that he had dreamed he was a butterfly, and felt in every respect exactly like a butterfly; and that he was not certain whether he was Chuang Tzu dreaming he was a butterfly, or a butterfly dreaming he was Chuang Tzu.

For a month or so, Karel Weissman and I tried to ' experiment with consciousness'. Over the Christmas holiday, we tried the experiment of staying awake for three days on black coffee and cigars. The result was certainly a remarkable intensity of intellectual perception. I remember saying: 'If I could live like this all the time, poetry would become worthless, because I can see so much further than any poet'. We also tried experiments with ether and carbon tetrachloride. In my own case, these were altogether less interesting. I certainly experienced some enormous feeling of insight – of the kind that one occasionally gets on the point of sleep – but it was very brief, and I could not remember it afterwards. The ether gave me a headache for days, so after two experiments I decided to give it up. Karel claimed that his own results corresponded to those of Daumal, with certain differences; I seem to remember he found the idea of rows of black dots extremely significant. But he also found the physical after-effects unsettling, and gave it up. Later, when he became an experimental psychologist, he was able to get mescalin and lysergic acid for the asking, and suggested several times that I should try them. But by this time I had other interests, and refused. I shall speak of these 'other interests' presently.

This long parenthesis has been necessary to explain why I thought I understood Karel Weissman's last request to me. I am an archaeologist, not a psychologist. But I was his oldest friend, and I had once shared his interest in the problems of the outer-limits of human consciousness. In his last moments, surely his thoughts had returned to our long nights of talk at Uppsala, to the endless lagers we had consumed in the little restaurant overlooking the river, to the bottles of schnapps drunk in my room at two in the morning? Something about it all bothered me, some faint, indefinable anxiety, of the kind that had made me ring Karel's Hampstead house at midnight. But now there was nothing I could do about it; so I preferred to forget it. I was in the Hebrides

14

at the time of my friend's funeral – I had been called to examine the neolithic remains so remarkably preserved on Harris – and upon my return I found several filing cabinets of material on the landing outside my flat. My head was full of thoughts of neolithic man; I glanced into the first drawer, looked into a folder entitled: ' The Perception of Colour in Emotionally Starved Animals', and hastily slammed the drawer. Then I went into my flat and opened the *Archaeological Journal,* and came upon Reich's article on the electronic dating of the basalt figurines of the Boghazköy temple. My excitement was intense; I rang Spence at the British Museum, and rushed over to see him. For the next forty-eight hours I thought and ate and breathed nothing but Boghazköy figurines and the distinguishing features of Hittite sculpture.

This, of course, saved my life. There can be no possible doubt that the Tsathogguans were awaiting my return, waiting to see what I did. And luckily, my head was full of archaeology. My mind was floating gently in the immense seas of the past, lulled in the currents of history. Psychology was repellent to it. If I had eagerly studied my friend's material, searching for a clue to his suicide, my own mind would have been possessed and then destroyed within hours.

When I think of it now, I shudder. I was surrounded by evil, alien minds. I was like some diver at the bottom of the sea, so absorbed in contemplating the treasure of a sunken ship that I failed to notice the cold eyes of the octopus that lay in wait behind me. In other moods, I might have noticed them, as I did later at Karatepe. But Reich's discoveries occupied all my attention. It pushed out of my head all sense of duty to the memory of my dead friend.

I conclude that I was under fairly constant observation from the Tsathogguans for several weeks. It was during this time that I realized I must return to Asia Minor if I was to clear up the problems raised by Reich's criticisms of my own dating. Again, I can only feel that this decision was providential. It must have confirmed the Tsathogguans in the feeling that they had absolutely nothing to fear from me. Obviously, Karel had made a mistake; he could hardly have chosen a less suitable executor. In fact, I felt twinges of conscience about those filing cabinets during my remaining weeks in England, and once or twice forced myself to glance into them. On each occasion, I felt the same distaste for these matters of psychology, and closed them again. On the last occasion on which I did so, I remember wondering whether it would not be simpler to ask the caretaker to burn all this stuff in the basement furnace. The idea instantly struck me as utterly immoral, and I rejected it – a little surprised, to be honest, to find myself entertaining it. I had no idea that it was not ' I ' who thought the thought.

I have often wondered since then how far the choice of myself as executor was a part of my friend's design, and how far it was a last minute decision made in despair. Obviously, he can have given little thought to it, or they would have known. Was it, then, a sudden inspired decision, the last lightning flash of one of the most brilliant minds of the 20th century? Or was I chosen *faute de mieux*? We may know the answer one day if we can obtain access to the Tsathogguans' archives. I like to think that the choice was intentional, a masterstroke of cunning. For if providence was on his side in making the choice, it was certainly on mine during the next six months, when I thought of anything but Karel Weissman's papers.

When I left for Turkey, I instructed my landlord that Baumgart was to be allowed into my flat during my absence. He had agreed to attempt a preliminary sorting of the papers. I had also opened negotiations with two American publishers of textbooks of psychology, who showed themselves interested in Karel Weissman's papers. Then, for some months, I thought no more about psychology, for the problems involved in the dating of the basalt figurines absorbed my full attention. Reich had established himself in the laboratories of the

Turkish Uranium Company at Diyarbakir. His main concern so far, of course, had been the dating of human and animal remains by the argon method, and in this technique he had become the foremost world authority. In turning his attention from the ages of prehistory to the reign of the Hittites, he was exploring a relatively new field as far as his own work was concerned. Man is a million years old; the Hittite invasion of Asia Minor occurred in 1,900 BC. For this reason, he was delighted to see me in Diyarbakir, for my own book on the civilization of the Hittites had been the standard work since its publication in 1980.

For my own part, I found Reich a fascinating man. My own mind is at home in any period from 2,500 BC to the end of the tenth century AD. Reich's mind was at home in any period from the Carboniferous age onward, and he could speak of the Pleistocene – a mere million years ago – as if it were recent history. I was present once when he examined a dinosaur tooth, and he remarked casually that it could not possibly be as recent as the Cretaceous age – that he would place it in the late Triassic – about fifty million years earlier. I was also present when a Geiger counter verified his guess. His instinct for this kind of thing was quite uncanny.

Since Reich will play a considerable part in this story, I should say something about him. Like myself, he was a big man; but unlike myself, his bigness owed nothing to surplus fat. He had the shoulders of a wrestler, and an enormous, prognathous jaw. His voice always gave surprise, for it was gentle and rather high – the result, I believe, of a throat infection in childhood.

But the main difference between myself and Reich lay in our emotional attitude towards the past. Reich was a scientist through and through. For him, figures and measurements were everything; he could derive enormous pleasure from reading through a column of Geiger readings that extended over ten pages. His favourite assertion was that history should be a science. Now I have never tried to hide the powerful element of the romantic in my composition. I became an archaeologist through an almost mystical experience. I had been reading a volume on the civilization of Nineveh by Layard, which I had picked up casually in the bedroom of the farm at which I was staying. Some of my clothes were drying on a line in the yard, and a burst of thunder made me hurry outside to get them in. Just inside the farmyard there was a large pool of grey water, rather muddy. As I was taking the clothes from the line, my mind still in Nineveh, I happened to notice this pool, and forgot, for a moment, where I was or what I was doing there. As I looked at it, the puddle lost all familiarity and became as alien as a sea on Mars. I stood staring at it, and the first drops of rain fell from the sky, and wrinkled its surface. At that moment I experienced a sensation of happiness and of insight such as I had never known before. Nineveh and all history suddenly became as real and as alien as that pool. History became such a *reality* that I felt a kind of contempt for my own existence, standing there with my arms full of clothes. For the remainder of that evening I walked around like one in a dream. From then on, I knew I had to devote my life to ' digging up the past ', and to trying to reconstitute that vision of reality.

It will be seen, in a moment, that all this has great relevance to my story. It meant that Reich and I had totally dissimilar attitudes towards the past, and constantly amused one another by minor revelations of our individual temperaments. For Reich, science contained all the poetry of life, and the past merely happened to be the field in which he exercised his ability. As to myself, science was a servant of poetry. My earliest mentor, Sir Charles Myers, had strengthened this attitude in me, for he had the most total contempt for all that was modern. To see him working on a digging was to see a man who had ceased to exist in the twentieth century, and who looked down on history like a golden eagle from some mountain peak. He had a shuddering distaste for most human beings; he once complained to me that most of

18

them seemed 'so unfinished and shabby'. Myers made me feel that the true historian is a poet rather than a scientist. He once said that the contemplation of individual men made him dream of suicide, and that he could reconcile himself to being human only by considering the rise and fall of civilizations.

During those first weeks at Diyarbakir, when the rainy season made it impossible for us to do field work on the Karatepe diggings, we had many long discussions during the evenings, while Reich drank beer by the pint and I drank a most excellent local brandy. (Even here the differences in our temperaments revealed themselves!)

Now it happened that one evening, I received a letter from Baumgart. It was very brief. He stated simply that he had discovered certain papers in Weissman's filing cabinets that convinced him that Weissman had been insane for some time before his suicide: that Weissman had believed that ' they ' were aware of his efforts, and would try to destroy him. Baumgart said that it was clear from the context that ' they ' did not refer to human beings. He had therefore decided not to go ahead with his negotiations for the publication of Weissman's psychological papers; he would leave it for my return.

Naturally, I was puzzled and intrigued. It happened that Reich and I had reached a certain point in our work where we felt we had a right to rest and congratulate ourselves; so our talk that evening was concerned entirely with Weissman's ' madness ' and suicide. During the early part of the discussion, there were also present two of Reich's Turkish colleagues from Izmir, and one of them mentioned the curious fact that the suicide rate in the *rural areas* of Turkey had risen in the past ten years. This surprised me; for while the urban suicide rate had increased steadily in most countries, the country populations, on the whole, seemed immune from the virus.

This led one of our guests, Dr Omer Fu'ad, to tell us about

the researches that his department had been conducting into the suicide rate of the ancient Egyptians and Hittites. The later Arzawa tablets mention an epidemic of suicide in the reign of King Mursilis the Second (1334-1306 BC), and give the figures for Hattusas. Strangely enough, the Menetho papyri, discovered in 1990 in the monastery at Es Suweida, also mention an epidemic of suicide in Egypt in the reign of Haremhab and Sethos the First, covering approximately the same period (1350-1292 BC). His companion, Dr Muhammed Darga, was an admirer of that strange piece of historical charlatanism, Spengler's *Decline of the West*, and proceeded to argue that such epidemics of suicide could be predicted accurately according to the age of the civilization and its degree of urbanization. He went on to evolve some far-fetched metaphor about biological cells and their tendency to 'die voluntarily' when the body has lost its ability to be stimulated by the environment.

Now all this struck me as nonsense, since the civilization of the Hittites was barely 700 years old in 1350 B.C., while that of the Egyptians was at least twice as old. And Dr Darga had a rather dogmatic manner of stating his 'facts' that annoyed me. I became rather heated – the brandy may have had something to do with it – and challenged our guests to produce facts and figures. They said, very well, they would – and would submit them to the judgment of Wolfgang Reich. And, having to fly back to Izmir, they took their leave fairly early.

Now Reich and I engaged in a discussion that sticks in my mind as the true beginning of the story of the fight against the mind parasites. Reich, with his clear, scientific intelligence, quickly summarized the pros and cons of our earlier arguments, and allowed that Dr Darga seemed to have little gift for scientific detachment. Reich then went on:

'Consider the facts and figures that are available to us about our own civilization. How much do they actually tell us? These suicide figures, for example. In 1960, a hundred and ten people of every million committed suicide in England – a doubling of the rate since a century earlier. By 1970, this rate had doubled again, and by 1980, it had multiplied by six ...'

Reich had an astonishing mind; he seemed to have stored all the important statistics of the century in it. Now usually, I detest figures. But as I listened to him, something happened to me. I felt a touch of coldness inside me, as if I had suddenly become aware of the eyes of some dangerous creature. It passed in a moment, but I found myself shuddering. Reich asked: ' Cold?' I shook my head. And when Reich stopped talking for a while, to stare out of the window at the lighted street below us, I found myself saying:

' When all's been said, we know almost nothing about human life.'

He said cheerfully: ' We know enough to be getting on with, and that's all you can expect.'

But I could not forget that feeling of coldness. I said:

' After all, civilization is a kind of dream. Supposing a man suddenly woke up from that dream? Wouldn't it be enough to make him commit suicide?'

I was thinking about Karel Weissman, and he knew it. He said:

' But what about these delusions about monsters?'

I had to agree that this failed to fit my theory. But I could not shake off the cold touch of depression that had settled on me. What is more, I was now definitely afraid. I felt that I had seen something that I could not forget – to which I would have to return. And I felt that I could easily slide downhill into a state of nervous terror. I had drunk half a bottle of brandy, yet now I felt horribly sober, coldly aware that my body was slightly drunk, yet unable to identify with it. The idea that came to me was terrible. It was that the suicide rate was increasing because thousands of human beings were ' awakening ', like me, to the absurdity of human life, and simply refused to go on. The dream of history was coming to an end. Mankind was already starting to wake up; one day it would wake up properly, and there would be mass suicide.

These thoughts were so awful that I was tempted to go back to my room and brood on them. Yet I forced myself, against my will, to express them to Reich. I don't think he fully understood me, but he saw that I was in a dangerous condition, and with inspired insight, he said the exact words that were necessary to restore my peace of mind. What he began to talk about was the strange part that coincidence had played in archaeology; coincidence that would be too wild to use in fiction. He talked of how George Smith had journeyed from London with the absurd hope of finding the clay tablets that would complete the epic of Gilgamesh, and how he had, in fact, found them. He talked of the equally 'impossible' story of Schliemann's discovery of Troy, of Layard's finding of Nimrud – as if some invisible thread of destiny had pulled them towards their discovery. I had to admit that, more than any other science, archaeology inclines one to believe in miracles.

He followed it up swiftly. ' But if you can agree with that, then surely you must see that you're mistaken in thinking that civilization is a kind of dream – or a nightmare? A dream appears to be logical while it lasts, but when we wake up we see that it had no logic. You are suggesting that our illusions impose a similar logic on life. Well, the stories of Layard, Schliemann, Smith, Champollion, Rawlinson, Bossert, contradict you flatly. They really happened. They are real life stories that make use of outrageous coincidence in a way that no novelist would risk . . .'

He was right, and I had to agree. And when I thought of that strange destiny that had guided Schliemann to Troy, Layard to Nimrud, I recollected similar examples from my own life – for example, of my first major ' find ' – of the parallel texts in Phoenician, proto-Hattian and Kanisic at Kadesh. I can still remember my overwhelming sense of destiny, of some 'divinity that shapes our ends' – or at least, in some mysterious law of chance – that came over me as I scraped the earth from those clay tablets. For I *knew*, at least half an hour before I found those texts, that I was going to make a remarkable discovery that day; and when I stuck in my spade in a casually chosen spot, I had no fear that it would prove to be a waste of time.

In less than ten minutes, Reich had talked me back into a state of optimism and sanity.

I did not know it, but I had won my first battle against the Tsathogguans.

(Editor's note: from this point onward, the tape recording has been supplemented by Professor Austin's Autobiographical Notes, by kind permission of the Librarian of Texas University. These notes have been published separately by the University in Professor Austin's *Miscellanies*. I have attempted to use the notes only to expand material mentioned in the tape recording, which continues for another ten thousand words or so.)

The luck of the god of Archaeology was certainly with me that spring. Reich and I worked together so well that I decided to take a flat in Diyarbakir and remain there for at least a year. And in April, a few days before we set out for the Black Mountain of Karatepe, I received a letter from Standard Motors and Engineering, Karel Weissman's former employers, saying that they would like to return a great many of Weissman's papers to me, and enquiring as to my present whereabouts. I replied that letters would reach me care of the Anglo-Indian Uranium Company at Diyarbakir, and that I would be grateful if they would return Weissman's papers to my London address, or to Baumgart, who was still in Hampstead.

When Professor Helmuth Bossert first approached Kadirli, the nearest 'town' to the Black Mountain of the Hittites, in 1946, he had a difficult journey over muddy roads. In those days, Kadirli was a tiny provincial town with no electricity. Today it is a comfortable but quiet little town with two excellent hotels, and within an hour's reach of London by rocket plane. The trip from there to the Black Mountain, Karatepe, cost Bossert another arduous day's travel over shepherds' paths overgrown with prickly broom. We, in our own helicopter, reached Kadirli in an hour from Diyarbakir, and Karatepe in a further twenty minutes. Reich's electronic equipment had already been brought by transport plane forty-eight hours earlier.

I should, at this point, say something about the purpose of our expedition. There are many mysteries attached to the ' Black Mountain ', which is part of the Anti-Taurus mountain range. The so-called Hittite Empire collapsed in about 1200 BC, overcome by hordes of barbarians, prominent among whom were the Assyrians. Yet the Karatepe remains date from five hundred years later, as do those at Carchemish and Zinjirli. What happened in those five hundred years? How did the Hittites succeed in preserving so much of their culture through such a turbulent time, when its northern capital – Hattusas – was in the hands of the Assyrians? This was the problem to which I had devoted ten years of my life.

I had always believed that further clues might lie deep under the ground, in the heart of the Black Mountain – just as deep excavations into a mound at Boghazköy had revealed tombs of a highly civilized people a thousand years older than the Hittites. My excavations in 1987 had, in fact, turned up a number of strange basalt figurines, whose carving differed strikingly from the Hittite sculptures found on the surface – the famous bulls, lions and winged sphinxes. They were flat and angular; there was something barbaric about them – and yet not in the manner of African sculptures, with which they have occasionally been compared. The cuneiform symbols on these figures were distinctively Hittite, rather than Phoenician or Assyrian, yet, if it had not been for these, I would have guessed that the figures came from a completely different culture. The hieroglyphs in themselves presented another problem. Our knowledge of the Hittite language has been fairly comprehensive since the researches of Hrozny, yet there are still many lacunae. These tend to occur in texts dealing with religious ritual. (We could imagine, for example, some archaeologist of a future civilization being baffled by a copy of the Catholic mass, with its sign of the cross and odd abbreviations.) In that case, we surmised, the symbols on the basalt figures must deal almost entirely with religious ritual, for about seventy-five per cent of them were unknown to us. One of the few statements we could read was: 'Before (or below) Pitkhanas dwelt the great old ones'. Another read: 'Tudaliyas paid homage to Abhoth the Dark'. The Hittite symbols for 'dark' may also signify 'black', 'unclean' or 'untouchable' in the Hindu sense.

My finds had excited considerable comment in the world of archaeology. My own first view was that the figurines belonged to another proto-Hattian culture (i.e. the forerunners of the Hittites), that differed considerably from the one discovered at Boghazköy, and from which the Hittites took over their cuneiform. Pitkhanas was an early Hittite ruler of about 1900 BC. If my surmise was correct, then the inscription meant that before Pitkhanas there lived the great proto-Hattians from whom the Hittites derived their script. ('Below' could also signify that their tombs were below those of the Hittites, as at Boghazköy.) As to the reference to Tudaliyas, another Hittite ruler of about 1700 BC, it again seemed likely that the Hittites had derived some of their religious ritual from the proto-Hattians, of whom 'Abhoth the Dark' (or unclean) was a god.

This, I say, was my original interpretation: that the Hittites had taken over parts of the religion of their predecessors at Karatepe, and had made inscriptions upon Hattian figurines to this effect. But the more I considered the evidence (which is too complex to detail here), the more I was inclined to believe that the figurines helped to explain how Karatepe remained an island of culture long after the fall of the Hittite empire. What force will keep invaders at bay over a long period? Not, in this case, the force of arms; the evidence at Karatepe reveals an artistic, not a military culture. Sheer indifference? Why should they be indifferent? Through Karatepe, Zinjirli and Carchemish lay the road to the south, to Syria and Arabia. No; it seemed to me there was only one force strong enough to hold back an ambitious and warlike nation: superstitious fear. Surely the power of Karatepe and its neighbours was the power of some mighty religion – some religion of magic? Possibly Karatepe was a recognized centre of magical culture, like Delphi. Hence those strange reliefs of bird-headed men, of strange, beetle-like creatures, of winged bulls and lions?

Reich disagreed with me, and his disagreement was based upon his dating of the figurines. He claimed that, in spite of their excellent state of preservation, they were many thousands of years older than the proto-Hattian culture. He later verified this beyond all doubt with the use of his ' neutron dater '. Well, I was willing to be corrected; I was not entirely happy with my own provisional dating of the figurines. But an immense problem remained. As far as we know, there was *no civilization whatever* in Asia Minor before 3000 BC Further south, civilization dates back to 5000 BC; but not in Turkey. So who made the figurines, if not the proto-Hattians? Did they come from further south? If so, where?

During the first two months that I spent with him, Reich continued to work on his ' neutron dater ', and used my figurines as basic testing material. But here absurd difficulties arose. The dater showed itself remarkably accurate with samples of potsherd from Sumer and Babylon, where we had means of cross-checking its results. But they had little success with the figurines. At least, their results were so extraordinary as to be obviously inaccurate. The neutron beam was directed at minute fragments of stone dust in the cracks and hollows of the figurines. From the ' weathering ' and decay of these fragments, the dater should have been able to give us a rough estimate of how long ago the basalt was carved. It failed completely; the needle of the indicator swung to its furthest limit – about 10,000 BC! Reich talked about increasing the range of the indicator, simply out of curiosity, to see what date it would finally arrive at. In fact, he actually doubled its range, by some fairly simple adjustments. The needle still swung to its limit with the same unhesitating speed. It was becoming insane, and Reich began to wonder if he had made some elementary error. Perhaps the dust had not been produced by carving? – in which case, the dater was attempting to give us the age of the basalt itself! At all events, Reich left his assistants the task of constructing a dial that would show anything up to a million years – an immense task that would take most of the summer. And then we made our expedition to Karatepe, to try to investigate the problem at its source.

Yes . . . the source of the problem. How incredible it now seems as I tell the story! How is it possible to believe in simple ' coincidence ' in the light of these facts? For my two ' problems ' were converging: the problem of my friend's suicide, and the problem of the basalt figurines. When I think back upon that summer, it is impossible to believe in a materialistic historical determinism.

Let me try to place the events in their order. We arrived at Kadirli on April 16th. On the 17th, we established a camp at Karatepe. Admittedly, there was nothing to stop us from commuting between Karatepe and our comfortable hotel at Kadirli. But our workmen had to stay in the nearest village, and we decided that it might be better if we spent most of our time at the site of the excavation. Besides, all the romantic in me revolted at the idea of leaving the second millenium BC and plunging back into the late twentieth century every evening. So we set up our tents on a level space of ground near the top of the mound. From below us came the perpetual roar of the Pyramus river, with its swirling yellow waters. The electronic probe was set up on top of the mound.

I should say a word about this instrument: Reich's invention, that has since revolutionized the science of archaeology. Fundamentally it is no more than an X-ray, whose principle is similar to that of the mine detector. But a mine detector is only able to detect metal, and an X-ray will only be stopped by some hard, opaque body. Since the earth itself is hard and opaque, the old X-ray principle was of no use in archaeology. Moreover, the things that interest archaeologists – stones, earthenware and the rest – have more or less the same molecular structure as the surrounding earth, so they would hardly show up on an X-ray plate.

Reich's modification of the electronic laser would penetrate to a depth of three miles, and its principle of 'neutron feedback' meant that it immediately indicated any object of regular shape – a stone slab, for example. The only problem then was to dig down to the object, and this could be done fairly easily with our robot 'moles'.

It should not be difficult to imagine my state of excitement on the day we set out for Karatepe. Fifteen years of hard digging had failed to reveal any more basalt figurines, or to yield any clue to their source. The sheer volume of earth to be excavated made the problem apparently insoluble. Reich's invention solved it with a beautiful simplicity.

And yet, for the first three days, the results were disappointing. A probe taken directly below the old diggings revealed nothing. A further half day was occupied in moving the probe to another site a hundred yards away. This time I was certain that something would be revealed – and I was mistaken. Reich and I looked gloomily at the plain below us, then at the enormous bulk of the electronic probe, and wondered how many times it would have to be moved before we made a 'find'.

On the third evening, we received a visit from our two Turkish colleagues, Fu'ad and Darga. We decided to fly back into Kadirli for a meal at the hotel. Our feelings of irritability – due to our suspicion that they were there to spy on us for the Turkish government – soon vanished, for they were both full of warmth, sympathy and eager questionings. After an excellent meal and some good claret, the day's disappointments seemed less important. Afterwards, we retired to the visitors' lounge, which we had to ourselves, and drank Turkish coffee and brandy. It was at this point that Dr Muhammed Darga revived the topic of suicide. He had come armed with facts and figures this time. I shall not attempt to detail the discussion that followed – it went on until well after midnight – but it certainly seemed to indicate that Darga's theories about 'biological decay' were not as wild as they sounded. How, said Darga, could we account for this tremendous rise in the world suicide rate if we stuck to our view that it was simply a matter of 'civilization neurosis'? Too much security, lack of real purpose? But there was still plenty of 'challenge' in the modern world, and psychology had made tremendous advances in the past fifty years. The crime rate was far below what we might expect from the world's overcrowding. In the first half of the twentieth century, the crime rate and the suicide rate had risen together. So why had the crime rate dropped while the suicide rate had increased so dramatically? It wasn't good sense. Suicide and crime had always been connected in the past. In the first half of the twentieth century, the high suicide rate was partly due to crime, since one third of all murderers committed suicide. No, said Darga, this was a matter of some strange law of historical decay that only Spengler had suspected. Individual men are merely the cells in the great body of civilization; and, as with the human body, the rate of decay increases steeply with age . . .

I had to admit that he had me more than half convinced. At half past midnight, the four of us parted on the best of terms, and our two helicopters separated in the moonlight above Kadirli. We were back at the excavation by one o'clock.

It was a beautiful night. The air was full of the scent of asphodel, which the Greeks called the flower of the underworld, and of the distinctive odour of the shrubs that grew over the hill. The only sound was the churning of the river. The mountain peaks reminded me of my first trip to the moon; they had the same detached, dead beauty.

Reich went into his tent; he was still brooding on Darga's statistics. I walked up the hill, and into one of the chambers of the upper gate. Then I climbed the stairs to the top of the wall, and stood there looking out over the moonlit plain. I admit that my mood was romantic, and that I experienced a need to intensify it. So I stood there, hardly breathing, thinking of the dead sentries who had stood where I now stood, and of the days when only the Assyrians lay on the other side of those mountains.

All at once, my thoughts took a gloomy turn. I felt totally insignificant, meaningless, standing there. My life was the tiniest ripple on the sea of time. I felt the alienness of the world around me, the indifference of the universe, and a kind of wonder at the absurd persistency of human beings whose delusions of grandeur are incurable. Suddenly it seemed that life was no more than a dream. For human beings, it never became a reality.

The loneliness was unbearable. I wanted to go and talk to Reich, but the light in his tent had gone out. I felt in my upper pocket for a handkerchief, and my hand encountered a cigar that I had accepted from Dr Fu'ad. I had taken it as a ritual gesture of friendliness, for I am almost a non-smoker. Now its smell seemed to take me back to the human world, and I decided to light it. I cut off its end with a penknife, and pierced the other end. As soon as I took the first mouthful of smoke, I regretted it. It tasted foul. I placed it on the wall beside me, and continued to stare out over the valley. After a few minutes, its pleasant smell led me to take it up again. This time I took several more deep pulls at it, swallowing the smoke. My forehead felt damp, and I had to lean on the wall. For a while I was afraid I was about to vomit and waste my excellent supper. Then the nausea passed, but the feeling of disembodiment persisted.

At this point, I looked at the moon again – and was suddenly overwhelmed with an inexpressible fear. I felt like a sleepwalker who wakes up and finds himself balancing on a ledge a thousand feet above the ground. The fear was so immense that I felt as if my mind would dissolve; it seemed impossible to bear. I tried hard to fight it, to understand its cause. It was connected with this world I was looking at – with the realization that I was a mere object in a landscape. This is extremely difficult to make clear. But I suddenly seemed to see that men manage to stay sane because they see the world from their own tiny, intensely personal viewpoint, from their worm's eye view. Things impress them or frighten them, but they still see them from behind this windshield of personality. Fear makes them feel less important, but it does not negate them completely; in a strange way, it has the opposite effect, for it intensifies their feeling of personal existence. I suddenly seemed to be taken out of my personality, to see myself as a mere item in a universal landscape, as unimportant as a rock or fly.

This led to the second stage of the experience. I said to myself: ' But you are far more than a rock or a fly. You are not a mere object. Whether it is an illusion or not, your mind contains knowledge of all the ages. *Inside* you, as you stand here, there is more knowledge than in the whole of the British Museum, with its thousand miles of bookshelves '.

This thought, in a sense, was new to me. It led me to forget the landscape, and to turn my eyes inside myself. And a question presented itself. If space is infinite, how about the space *inside* man? Blake said that eternity opens from the centre of an atom. My former terror vanished. Now I saw that I was mistaken in thinking of myself as an object in a dead landscape. I had been assuming that man is limited because his brain is limited, that only so much can be packed into the portmanteau. But the the spaces of the mind are *a new dimension*. The body is a mere wall between two infinities. Space extends to infinity outwards; the mind stretches to infinity inwards.

It was a moment of revelation, of overwhelming insight. But as I stood there, totally oblivious of the outside world, straining all my powers to stare into those inner spaces, something happened that terrified me. This is almost impossible to describe. But it seemed that, out of the corner of my eye – the eye of attention that was turned inward – I caught a *movement* of some alien creature. It was a strange shock, the feeling you would get if you were relaxed in a warm bath, and you suddenly felt a slimy movement against your leg.

In a moment, the insight had passed. And as I looked at the mountain peaks above me, and at the moon sailing over them, I felt a thrill of pleasure, as if I had just returned home from the other end of the universe. I felt dizzy and very tired. All this had taken less than five minutes. I turned and walked back to my tent, and tried to look inside myself again. For a moment, I succeeded.

This time, I felt nothing.

But when I was wrapped up in my sleeping bag, I found that I no longer wanted to sleep. I would have preferred to talk to Reich, or to anyone. I had to express what I had suddenly realized. Man assumes that his inner world is private. ' The grave's a fine and private place ' said Marvell, and we have the same feeling about the mind. In the real world, our freedom is limited; in imagination, we can do anything we like; what is more, we can defy the world to penetrate the secret; the mind is the most private place in the universe –

sometimes, perhaps, too private. ' We each think of the key, each in his prison'. And the whole difficulty of treating madmen is to break into that prison.

Yet I could not forget that feeling of something *alien* inside my mind. Now I thought back on it, it did not seem so terrifying. After all, if you walk into your own room, expecting it to be empty, and you find someone there, your first response is fear: it could be a burglar. But this soon passes. Even if it *is* a burglar, you confront him as a reality, and that original flash of fear passes away. What was so alarming was that feeling of something – or someone – inside my own head, so to speak.

As my mind lost its fear, and became simply interested in the problem, I felt sleepy. One of my last thoughts before I fell asleep was to wonder if this was some kind of hallucination due to the Turkish coffee and the cigar.

When I woke at seven the next morning, I knew it wasn't. The memory of that sensation was curiously clear. And yet, let me confess, it now aroused a kind of excitement in me rather than terror. This should be easy enough to understand. The everyday world demands our attention, and prevents us from ' sinking into ourselves '. As a romantic, I have always resented this; I like to sink into myself. The problems and anxieties of living make it difficult. Well, now I had an anxiety that referred to something *inside* me, and it reminded me that my inner world was just as real and important as the world around me.

At breakfast, I was tempted to talk to Reich about it all. Something withheld me – the fear, I suppose, that he would simply fail to understand. He remarked that I seemed abstracted, and I said that I'd made the mistake of smoking Darga's cigar – and that was all.

That morning, I supervised the moving of the electronic probe to a place further down the mound. Reich went back to his tent to try to devise some easier method for moving the thing – a cushion of air underneath, for example, on the

B

hovercraft principle. The workmen shifted the probe to a position halfway down the mound, below the lower gate. Then, when it was ready, I took my seat, adjusted the controls on the screen, and pulled the starter.

Almost instantly, I knew I had struck something. The white line that ran from the top to the bottom of the screen showed a distinct bulge halfway down. When I cut the power, increasing the feedback, this immediately spread into parallel horizontal lines. I sent the foreman to fetch Reich, and proceeded to move the control cautiously, probing around the regular object in all directions. The screen showed that there were more of these objects to the left and right of it.

This, of course, was my first experience of discovering anything with the probe, so I had no idea of the size of the object I had found, or of its depth below the ground. But when Reich came running over a moment later, he took one look at the dial, another at the controls, and said: 'Oh Christ, the bloody thing's gone wrong.'

'In what way?'

'You must have twisted the control too far, and disconnected something. According to this, the object you've located is two miles below the ground and seventy feet high!'

I climbed off the seat rather ruefully. It is true that I have no ability to deal with mechanical appliances. New cars break down within hours when I drive them; machines that have never given the slightest trouble blow a fuse as soon as I approach. In this case, I had no consciousness of having done anything wrong, but I felt guilty all the same.

Reich unscrewed a plate and looked inside. He said there was nothing obviously wrong, and that he would have to test all the circuits after lunch. When I apologized, he slapped me on the shoulder.

'Never mind. We've found something anyway. Now all we've got to discover is how deep it lies.'

We ate a good cold lunch. Then Reich rushed off to his machine. I took an air mattress, and went and lay down in the shadow of the lion gate, to make up for lost sleep. And I slept deeply and peacefully for two hours.

When I opened my eyes, I saw Reich standing beside me, staring out across the river. I looked at my watch, and sat up hastily.

'Why on earth didn't you wake me?'

He sat down on the ground beside me. His manner struck me as subdued.

'What is it? Can't you trace the fault?'

He looked at me thoughtfully.

'There is no fault.'

I failed to understand.

'You mean it's repaired?'

'No. There never was any fault.'

'Well, that's cheering. What went wrong then?'

'That's what bothers me. Nothing went wrong.'

'No? In that case, you know how deep this thing is?'

'Yes. It's as deep as the gauge showed. Two miles.'

I restrained my excitement; stranger things had happened.

'Two miles,' I said. 'But that's quite a distance below the foundations of this hill. I mean . . . that kind of depth ought to take us down to archaeozoic rocks.'

'That depends. But I'm inclined to agree with you.'

'Besides, if it's accurate about the depth, it's presumably accurate about the size of the blocks – seventy feet high. That sounds a trifle unlikely. Even the building blocks of the great pyramid aren't that size.'

Reich said good-humouredly: 'My dear Austin, I agree with you completely. The thing is impossible. But I have checked every circuit in the machine. I don't see how I could be mistaken.'

'There's only one way to find out – send a mole down.'

'Which is what I was about to suggest. However, if it's really two miles down, the mole is of no use.'

'Why?'

'To begin with, because it was never intended to cut

through rock – only through earth or clay. It's bound to encounter rock at that depth. Second, because even if there's no rock at that depth, the pressure of the earth would destroy the mole – it would be like being two miles under the sea. The pressure would be thousands of pounds to the square inch. And since the temperature rises by a hundred degrees to a mile, it could also be too hot for its electrical equipment.

The sheer size of the problem now struck me. If Reich was correct, we could never hope to unearth the ' objects ' down there – objects that were obviously part of a wall of a city, or of a temple. With all our modern engineering efficiency, we had no machines capable of working at that temperature and pressure, and raising enormous blocks for two miles.

Reich and I returned to the probe, discussing this problem. If the probe was correct – and Reich seemed to think it was – then it set archaeology an extraordinary problem. How on earth could remains sink to this depth? Perhaps the whole tract of land had subsided in some eruption – collapsed into an abyss underneath? Then perhaps the hollow had been filled with water and mud . . . But mud to a depth of two miles! How many thousands of years would that take? We both felt as if we were going insane. It was a temptation to rush to the telephone and consult colleagues, but the fear of having made some absurd mistake held us back.

By five o'clock, we had the mole ready to launch, its nose pointing straight downwards. Reich operated the remote control panel, and its bullet-like nose began to revolve. Earth sprayed, then settled into a small, loose pile. For a few moments, the pile quivered. Then there was no sign of the mole.

I went across to the radar screen. At its top, a brilliant white dot seemed to tremble. As we watched, it moved down slowly – very slowly, slower than the minute hand of a watch. Next to the radar screen, a kind of television screen showed only wavy lines that looked as if they were made of smoke. Occasionally, these lines became thinner in places, or vanished altogether; this was when the mole encountered a rock. If it encountered any object that was more than ten feet across, it would stop automatically, and the electronic laser would scan its surface.

An hour later, the white dot had moved halfway down the screen – a depth of about a mile. It was now moving slower. Reich went to the probe, and set it going. Its screen registered the mole – at a mile down. And still in the same position, further down the screen showed the enormous blocks. The probe was accurate.

Now we all felt the tension. The workmen were standing in a group, their eyes fixed on the radar screen. Reich had switched off the probe, since its beam could damage the mole. We were risking damaging an expensive piece of equipment – yet we could see no alternative. We had checked and re-checked the probe. It indicated unmistakably that the immense blocks were of a more or less regular shape, and were resting side by side. It was impossible that they could be natural rocks.

Neither was it inevitable that we should lose the mole. Its electronically fortified metal would withstand a temperature of two thousand degrees; its makers had assumed that it might encounter veins of volcanic lava. The strength of its shell was enormous; the makers guaranteed that it could stand a pressure of two and a half tons to the square inch. But if it reached the blocks at a depth of two miles, it would be supporting about twice that weight, or very nearly. Besides, its transmitting equipment might not stand the temperature. And then there was always the possibility that it might pass beyond the range of the remote control, or sustain damage to its receiver.

By half past eight, night was falling, and the mole had traversed another half of the distance. The blocks were only half a mile below it. We had told the workmen to go home, but many of them stayed. Our cook prepared us a meal from tins; he was obviously in no condition to cook anything elaborate. When the night came down, we sat there in the dark, listening to the faint hum of the radar equipment, and watching the brilliant white dot. Sometimes, I became convinced that it had stopped. Reich, whose eyes were better than mine, assured me that it hadn't.

By half past ten, the last of the workmen had gone home. I had wrapped myself up in a dozen blankets, for the wind had risen. Reich chain-smoked; even I smoked two cigarettes. Suddenly, the humming stopped. Reich leapt to his feet. He said: ' It's there.'

' Are you sure?' I found that my voice had become a croak.

' Absolutely. The position's right. It's now directly over the blocks.'

' What now?'

' Now we activate the scanner.'

He started the machine again. Now our eyes were fixed on the television screen. It was blank, indicating that the scanner was trained on a massive and hard object. Reich adjusted the controls. The wavy lines began to reappear, but they were now thinner and straighter. Reich made some adjustment that brought them closer together, until the whole surface of the screen became a pattern of fine white and black lines, like a pair of pin-striped trousers. And showing very clearly against this pattern of lines there were a number of black scars, indentations in the rock. The excitement of the past few hours had been so great that I was able to look at these without strong emotion. It was impossible to doubt what they were. I had seen them many times before – on the basalt figurines. I was looking at the symbols that represented the name of Abhoth the Dark.

There was nothing more to be done. We photographed the screen, then went back to Reich's tent to radio Darga at Izmir. Within five minutes, Reich was speaking to him. He explained the situation, apologized for the risk we had taken with the mole – which belonged to the Turkish government – and told him that we had definitely established that these blocks belonged to the culture of the ' great old ones ' mentioned on one of the figurines.

Darga, I suspect, was a little drunk. The situation had to be explained to him at length before he understood. Then he proposed fetching Fu'ad and flying over to join us immediately. We convinced him there would be no point, as we were about to go to bed. He said that we should move the mole along to scan the next blocks. Reich pointed out that this was impossible. It could not move sideways, only forwards and backwards; it would have to be withdrawn a hundred feet or so, and re-directed. This would take several hours.

Finally, we convinced Darga, and broke the connection. We were both appallingly tired, yet neither of us felt like sleep. The cook had left equipment for making coffee. Against our better judgement, we used it, and opened a bottle of brandy.

It was there, sitting in Reich's tent at midnight, on the 21st of April, 1997, that I told Reich about my experience of the night before. I started to tell him, I think, to distract our minds from the problem of those seventy-foot blocks below the ground. In this, I succeeded. For, to my surprise, Reich found nothing strange in what I had to say. At university, he had studied the psychology of Jung, and was familiar with the idea of a ' racial unconscious '. If there was a racial unconscious, then human minds are not separate islands, but are all part of some great continent of mind. He had read a great deal more psychology than I had. He cited the work of Aldous Huxley, who had taken mescalin sometime in the 1940's, and had also reached my own conclusion that the mind stretches for infinity inside us. Huxley, apparently, had gone further, in a way, and spoken of the mind as a world of its own, like the world we live on – a planet with its own jungles and deserts and oceans. And on this planet – as one would expect – there live all kinds of strange creatures.

At this point, I objected. Surely Huxley's talk about strange creatures was only a metaphor, a piece of poetic licence? The 'inhabitants' of the mind are memories and ideas, not monsters.

At this, Reich shrugged.

'How do we know?'

'I agree, we don't. But it seems common sense.'

I thought about my experience of the night before, and felt less sure of myself. Was it 'common sense'? Or have we got into a habit of thinking about the human mind in a certain way – as our ancestors thought of the earth as the centre of the universe? I speak of 'my mind' as I speak of 'my back garden'. But in what sense is my back garden really 'mine'? It is full of worms and insects who do not ask my permission to live there. It will continue to exist after I am dead . . .

Oddly enough this train of thought had the effect of making me feel better. It explained my anxiety – or seemed to. If individuality is an illusion, and mind is actually a kind of ocean, why should it not contain alien creatures? Before falling asleep, I made a note to send for Aldous Huxley's *Heaven and Hell*. Reich's thoughts had taken a more practical turn. Ten minutes after we separated, he called to me from his tent: 'You know, I think we might be justified in asking Darga to lend us a large hovercraft for shifting the probe. It'd certainly make life easier . . .'

It now seems absurd that neither of us anticipated the consequences of our discovery. We expected, of course, to produce some excitement in archaeological circles. Both of us had conveniently forgotten the kind of thing that happened when Carter found the tomb of Tutankhamen, or when the Dead Sea scrolls were discovered at Qumran. Archaeologists are inclined to discount the world of mass communications and the hysteria of journalists.

Fu'ad and Darga woke us up at half past six, before the workmen arrived. They had with them four officials of the Turkish government, and a couple of American film stars who happened to be sightseeing. Reich was inclined to resent this unannounced intrusion, but I pointed out to him that the Turkish government was within its rights – except, perhaps, where the film stars were concerned.

First of all, they wanted to be convinced that the blocks were really two miles deep. Reich started the probe, and showed them the outline of the ' Abhoth block ' (as we came to refer to it), and the mole next to it. Darga expressed doubts that the mole could have penetrated to a depth of two miles. Patiently, Reich went over to the mole's transmission panel, and switched it on.

The result was discomforting. The screen remained blank. He tried the digging control; it produced no result. There could be only one conclusion: that the temperature – or possibly the pressure – had damaged the mole's equipment.

It was a setback, but not as serious as it might have been. A mole was expensive, but it could be replaced. But Darga and Fu'ad still wanted to be convinced that there was not some fault in the mechanism of the probe. Reich spent the morning demonstrating that every circuit was in order, and that there could be no room for doubt that the blocks were really two miles down. We developed the radar photograph of the Abhoth block, and compared its cuneiform with that of the basalt figurines. It was impossible to doubt that the two came from the same culture.

There was, of course, only one possible answer to the problem: a full scale tunnel down to the blocks. I should point out that, at this point, we had no idea of the size of individual blocks. We presumed that the height indicated on the probe's screen could be the height of a wall or a whole building. Admittedly, the radar photograph posed an interesting problem, for it had been taken from *above* – which meant, presumably, that the wall, or building, was lying on its side. No past civilization has ever been known to write inscriptions on the top of walls or on the roof of buildings.

Our visitors were baffled but impressed. Unless this turned out to be some kind of a freak, it would undoubtedly prove to be the greatest find in archaeological history. So far, the oldest civilization known to man is that of the Masma Indians of the Marcahuasi plateau in the Andes – 9,000 years old. But we now recalled the results of our tests on the basalt figurines with the neutron dater, which we had assumed to be inaccurate. They tended to support our assumption that we were now dealing with the remains of a civilization at least twice as old as that of the Marcahuasi.

Fu'ad and his colleagues stayed to lunch, and left at about two o'clock. By now, their excitement was affecting me, although I had an obscure feeling of irritation at allowing myself to be affected. Fu'ad promised to send us a hover-craft as quickly as possible, but mentioned that it might take several days. Until this arrived, we felt reluctant to move the probe by hand. It was obvious that we were going to receive a great deal more governmental support than we had expected, and there was no sense in wasting energy. We had a second mole, but it seemed pointless to risk it. So at half past two, we sat in the shadow of the lower gate, drank orange squash, and felt at a loose end.

Half an hour later, the first of the journalists arrived – the Ankara correspondent of the *New York Times*. Reich was furious. He assumed – incorrectly – that the Turkish government was seizing this opportunity for publicity. (We later discovered that the two film stars were responsible for informing the press.) Reich vanished into his tent, and I was left to entertain the journalist, a pleasant enough man who had read my book on the Hittites. I showed him the photograph, and explained the working of the probe. When he asked me what had happened to the mole, I said I had no idea. For all I knew, it had been sabotaged by troglodytes.

This, I am afraid, was the first of my mistakes. I made the second when he asked me about the size of the Abhoth block. I pointed out that we had no evidence that it was a *single* block, even though there appeared to be similar blocks on either side of it. It could be a religious monument in the shape of an enormous block, or perhaps a construction like the ziggurat at Ur. If it was a single block, then it would indicate that we were dealing with a civilization of giants.

To my surprise, he took me seriously. Did I subscribe to the theory that the world had once been inhabited by giants who had been destroyed by some great lunar catastrophe? I said that, as a scientist, it was my business to keep an open mind until definite evidence was produced. But was *this* evidence? he persisted. I replied that it was too early to say. He then asked me whether I would agree that such immense building blocks could have been moved by ordinary men – as in the case of the Gizeh pyramid or the Toltec sun pyramid at Teotihuacan. Still unsuspecting, I pointed out that the largest blocks of the Gizeh pyramid weigh twelve tons; a seventy foot block could weigh a thousand tons. But I agreed that we still had no real knowledge of how the stones of the Cheops pyramid – or those at Stonehenge, for that matter – had been moved; these ancient people may have possessed a far greater knowledge than we realize . . .

Before I had finished talking to the *New York Times* man, three more helicopters appeared. More journalists. By four o'clock, Reich had been persuaded to emerge from his tent, and was demonstrating the mechanism of the probe – with a bad grace. By six o'clock, we were both hoarse and weary. We escaped back to the hotel in Kadirli, and managed to eat a quiet supper. The manager had been told to refuse all telephone calls. But at nine o'clock, Fu'ad got through to us. He was waving a copy of the *New York Times*. The whole front page was devoted to the story of the ' World's Biggest Discovery Ever '. I was quoted as endorsing the theory that we had discovered the city of a race of giants. I was made to hint that these giants had also been magicians who had raised their thousand ton building blocks by some strange art that has now been forgotten. A well known colleague of mine gave his opinion that the pyramids of Egypt and ancient Peru could never have been built by any known method of engineering, and that this new discovery would surely prove it beyond all doubt. On the inside page of the newspaper, a popular writer on archaeology contributed an article called ' The Giants of Atlantis '.

I assured Fu'ad that I had never said anything about giants – at least, not in the context quoted. He promised to ring the *New York Times* and correct their account. Then I crept off to Reich's room to drink a final glass of brandy, leaving instructions that I was at home to no one – not even the Sultan of Turkey.

I think I have said enough to indicate why we were unable to return to the site for another week. The Turkish government supplied soldiers to guard our equipment; but they had no orders to keep visitors at bay, and the air above Karatepe swarmed with helicopters like wasps around jam. The hotels in Kadirli were jammed for the first time since they had been built. Reich and I had to stay in our rooms, or risk being accosted a hundred times an hour by cranks and sensation seekers. The Turkish government granted us the hovercraft within twelve hours, but it was impossible to use it. On the following day, the Carnegie Foundation granted us two million dollars for starting the tunnel, and the World Finance Committee produced another two million. Finally, the Turkish government agreed to build a forty foot wire enclosure around the Black Mountain, and they did this in less than a week, with some help from American and Russian Foundations. We were then able to return to work.

Inevitably, everything had changed. There were no more quiet siestas after lunch, or midnight talks in our tent. Soldiers stood guard all over the mound. Prominent archaeologists from every country in the world plagued us with questions and suggestions. The air buzzed with helicopters, which were prevented from landing by warning radio broadcasts from a hastily erected control tower – again a product of American and Russian co-operation.

Still, the compensations were considerable. A team of engineers harnessed the probe to the hovercraft, so that we could take instant readings over the most difficult terrain. The Turkish government provided us with two more moles, both specially reinforced. Money and equipment could be had for the asking – a situation to delight the heart of any archaeologist.

Within two days we had made a number of astonishing discoveries. First of all, the probe indicated that we had, in fact, discovered a buried city. Walls and building extended for over a mile in both directions. The Black Mountain of Karatepe appeared to be roughly above the centre of this city. And it was, indeed, a city of giants. The ' Abhoth block ' was not a building or a religious monument; it was a single building block, cut from solid basalt, the hardest kind of volcanic basalt. One of the reinforced moles actually cut off a fragment of the block, and brought it to the surface.

Yet a curious bad luck followed us. Within forty-eight hours, we lost one of the reinforced moles in the same manner as the first. It ceased to respond to signals at a depth of two miles. A week later, we lost the other mole in the same manner—half a million pounds worth of equipment buried at the bottom of a sea of earth. A careless operator lost control of the hovercraft, and allowed the probe to crash into a hut full of Turkish soldiers, killing eighteen. The probe was undamaged, but the newspapers, which were still in full cry, were not slow to draw parallels with the misfortunes of the Carter-Carnarvon expedition of 1922, the sensational stories of the ' curse of Tutankhamen'. A colleague, upon whose discretion I thought I could rely, reported my theory that the Hittites of Karatepe owed their survival to their reputations as magicians, and started a new wave of sensational stories.

It was at this point that the name of H.P. Lovecraft entered the story. Like the majority of my colleagues, I had never heard of Lovecraft, the writer of supernatural stories who died in 1937. For a long time after his death, a small ' Lovecraft cult ' had persisted in America, largely due to the advocacy of Lovecraft's friend, the novelist August Derleth. It was Derleth who now wrote to Reich, pointing out that the name of ' Abhoth the Unclean ' occurs in Lovecraft's work, and that he figures as one of the ' Great Old Ones '.

My first thought, when Reich showed me the letter, was that it was a hoax. We checked in a dictionary of literature, and discovered that Derleth was a well known American writer, now in his eighties. Lovecraft was not mentioned in the dictionary, but a call to the British Museum produced the information that he had also existed, and had written the books Derleth attributed to him.

There was a sentence in Derleth's letter that struck me. After admitting that he could not explain how Lovecraft could have known about ' Abhoth the Dark ' – since the name does not occur in any of the Hittite documents that were uncovered before 1937 – he added : ' Lovecraft always attached great importance to dreams, and often told me that the subjects of many of his stories occurred to him in dreams '.

' Another piece of evidence for your racial subconscious,' I commented to Reich. He suggested that it was more probably coincidence. Abbaddon is the destroying angel of Hebrew legend; the ' hoth ' ending is Egyptian. A god ' Abaoth ' is mentioned in certain Babylonian writings that Lovecraft might have seen. As to the ' great old ones ', the phrase is not so strange that it might not have occurred to a writer of supernatural fiction. ' Why drag in the racial subconscious?' said Reich, and I was inclined to agree with him.

A few days later, we changed our minds. The parcel of books sent by Derleth finally arrived. I opened a story called

'The Shadow out of Time' – and immediately came upon a description of immense stone blocks buried beneath the desert of Australia. At the same moment, Reich, who was sitting in the other armchair, gave an exclamation, and read aloud the sentence: 'The dweller in darkness is also known by the name Nyogtha'. Only the evening before, we had arrived at a tentative translation of the inscription on the Abhoth block: 'And the horses shall be brought two by two into the presence of Niogtha'. I then read Reich the description of the underground cities from 'The Shadow out of Time', the 'mighty basalt cities of windowless towers' built by the 'half-polypus elder race'.

There could no longer be any reasonable doubt that Lovecraft had, in some strange way, anticipated our discoveries. We wasted no time in speculating how this had come about: whether Lovecraft had somehow looked into the future – in the manner described by Dunne in his *Experiment with Time* – and seen the results of our investigations, or whether his dreaming mind had somehow penetrated these secrets buried below the earth in Asia Minor. This was irrelevant. The question that now presented itself to us was: how much of Lovecraft's work was mere literary invention, and how much was visionary 'second sight'?

It seemed strange to be neglecting our archaeological duties to study the works of a writer who had published most of his work in a pulp magazine called *Weird Tales*. We kept our secret as long as possible, giving it out that we were devoting our days to the study of the cuneiform inscriptions. We spent several days locked in Reich's room (which was larger than mine), reading steadily through the works of Lovecraft. When our meals arrived, we concealed the books under cushions and pored over photographs of inscriptions. By this time, we had learnt our lesson; we knew what would happen if any journalist discovered how we occupied our days. We had talked to Derleth on the telescreen – a friendly and courteous old gentleman with abundant white hair – and asked him to mention his discovery to no one. He agreed readily enough, but pointed out that there were still many readers of Lovecraft who were bound to stumble upon the same discovery.

The study of Lovecraft was, in itself, an interesting and pleasant occupation. He was a man of remarkable imagination. Reading his works in chronological order, we observed a gradual change of viewpoint.* The early stories tend to have a New England background, and deal with a fictional county called Arkham, with wild hills and sinister valleys. The inhabitants of Arkham seem to be mostly weird degenerates with a taste for forbidden pleasures and the conjuration of demons. Inevitably, a large number of them come to a violent end. But gradually, there is a change in the tone of Lovecraft's work. His imagination turns from the horrible to the awe-inspiring, to visions of tremendous aeons of time, of giant cities, of the conflict of monstrous and superhuman races. Except that he continues to write in the language of horror stories – no doubt with his market in mind – he might be considered one of the earliest and best exponents of science fiction. It was mostly with this latter ' science fiction period ' that we were concerned, (although this should not be taken too literally; a mention of ' Abhoth the Unclean ' occurs in one of his earliest Arkham stories).

What was most striking was that these ' cyclopean cities ' of the great old ones (not the polypus race, which they replaced) fitted what we now knew of our own underground city. According to Lovecraft, these cities had no stairs, only inclined planes, for their inhabitants were huge, cone-like creatures with tentacles; the base of the cone was ' fringed with a rubbery grey substance, which moved the whole entity through expansion and contraction '. The probe had revealed that this city below Karatepe had many inclined

* These remarks on Lovecraft are taken from 'Lovecraft and the Kadath Inscriptions', a lecture delivered by Dr Austin before the New York Historical Society on 18th June, 1999.

48

planes, but apparently no stairs. And its size certainly merited the adjective ' cyclopean '.

As can well be imagined, our underground city presented a problem that is almost new to archaeology. Layard's problem of excavating the immense mound of Nimrud was nothing compared to ours. Reich calculated that in order to expose the ruins to the light of day, we would have to move about forty billion tons of earth (using the American billion – a thousand million.) Obviously, this could never be done. An alternative would be to dig a series of wide tunnels down to the city, and create large chambers at the end of these tunnels. It would have to be a series, because we could never risk creating a chamber of any size. No metal known to man could be relied upon to support a roof two miles thick. This would mean that the city itself could never be exposed as a whole; but the use of the probe might show us which parts were best worth the trouble. Even the digging of a single tunnel would involve moving a hundred thousand tons of earth. Still, this was well within the range of possibility.

It took the press exactly one week to catch up with our discovery of Lovecraft. This was, perhaps, the greatest sensation since our original discovery. The newspapers went insane. After all the talk about giants, magicians and dark gods, this was all the story needed. So far, popular archaeologists, pyramid cranks and exponents of the world-ice theory had had a field day. Now it was the turn of the spiritualists, occultists and the rest. Someone wrote an article to demonstrate that Lovecraft had borrowed his mythology from Madame Blavatsky. Someone else declared that it was all part of a cabalistic tradition. Lovecraft suddenly became the most widely read writer in the world; his books sold by the million in every language. And many who read him were terrified, believing that we were about to disturb the ' great old ones ' in their underground tombs, and that the result would be the catastrophe that Lovecraft describes so powerfully in ' The Call of Cthulhu '.

The city of ' The Shadow Out of Time ' was unnamed, but in an early Lovecraft novel it is mentioned as ' Unknown Kadath '. The newspaper writers christened our underground city ' Kadath ', and the name stuck. And almost immediately, a madman in New York called Dalgleish Fuller announced the formation of an Anti-Kadath society, whose purpose was to prevent us from excavating Kadath and disturbing the Great Old Ones. It is indicative of the insanity of those times that it immediately gained a membership of half a million, which quickly increased to three millions. They adopted the motto: ' Sanity lies in the future; forget the past '. They bought advertising time on television, and hired respectable psychologists to declare that Lovecraft's visions were a straightforward example of the Extra-Sensory Perception that Rhine and his colleagues had demonstrated so convincingly at Duke University. In that case, Lovecraft's warnings should be heeded; if the ' Great Old Ones ' were disturbed, it might well be the end of the human race. Dalgleish Fuller was a crank with some organizing ability. He rented an enormous area of ground within five miles of Karatepe, and set up a camping site there. His followers were exhorted to take their annual holidays there, and to spend them creating a nuisance at Karatepe. The land was privately owned by a farmer who was glad to accept the immense sums they offered him, and the whole thing was arranged before the Turkish government could take action. Fuller had a gift for attracting cranky rich women, who poured funds into the movement. They bought helicopters that buzzed over the mound dragging sky-signs with anti-Kadath inscriptions on them. At night, the helicopters came and dumped rubbish at the site, so that when we arrived in the morning, it often took several hours to clear away the rotten fruit and vegetables and old tins. The campers made protest marches to the barbed wire twice a day, sometimes in columns of a thousand. It was six weeks before the United Nations could be persuaded to take action and send in troops. By this time,

Fuller had recruited five American senators to his party, and together they introduced a bill to ban further digging at Karatepe. They explained, of course, that they were not activated by superstitious fear, but by reverence for a long dead civilization: Had we the right, said they, to disturb the sleep of centuries? It is to the credit of the Senate that the bill was outvoted by an enormous majority.

And just when it seemed that the Anti-Kadath society was losing influence through its noisy excesses, the whole thing was given new impetus with the publication of the findings on Stanlislaw Perzynski and Mirza Din. The facts about these two are briefly as follows. Perzynski was a Pole, Mirza Din was a Persian; both died insane in the first decade of the twentieth century. Perzynski was the better documented of the two; he had gained a certain reputation with a biography of his grandfather, the Russian poet Nadson. He had also edited an edition of the supernatural stories of Count Potocki. In 1898, he published a curious book warning the human race that it was about to be taken over by a race of monsters from another world, who had built enormous cities under the ground. A year later, he was committed to an asylum. His papers included strange sketches that might have been intended for illustrations of Lovecraft's stories about Kadath: monstrous architecture with inclined planes and great angular towers. These were published in full by the Anti-Kadath society. The case of Mirza Din was more dubious. He was also a writer of apocalyptic visions, which seldom achieved publication. He also spent the last five years of his life in an asylum, writing warning letters to members of the Persian government about a race of monsters that plotted to overrun the earth. Mirza Din located his monsters somewhere in the jungles of central Africa, and described them as looking like huge slugs. Their enormous cities were built from their own slimy excretion, which hardened into a kind of stone.

Most of Mirza Din's insane letters had been destroyed, but the few that had survived showed a remarkable similarity in style to Perzynsky's letters, and his slugs were sufficiently like Lovecraft's cones to lend credibility to the claim that all three were describing the same vision of the 'Great Old Ones' and their city.

After the government's intervention, and the digging of the first tunnel, the activities of the Anti-Kadath society gradually diminished; but for a period of eighteen months, they succeeded in creating a considerable nuisance. Dalgleish Fuller was murdered by one of his own female disciples under strange circumstances.*

The first tunnel was completed exactly a year after our discovery of the Abhoth block. The digging of the tunnel had been undertaken by the Italian government, who used the same giant mole that had already been used in the construction of the tunnel between Scilla and Messina (in Sicily), and later between Otranto and Linguetta in Albania. The digging itself took only a few days, but the chief problem was to prevent the lower parts of the tunnel from collapsing. The block itself was as impressive as we had expected – sixty-eight feet high, thirty feet wide, ninety feet long, carved out of solid volcanic basalt. It became impossible to doubt that we were dealing with a race of giants or magicians. From the existence of the basalt figurines, I was inclined to doubt that they had been a race of giants; the figurines were too small. (It was not until ten years later that Mercer's dramatic discoveries in Tanzania revealed that these great cities were inhabited both by giants and by human beings, and that the giants were almost certainly the slaves of the human beings.)

The exact dating of the blocks remained a problem. According to Lovecraft, the 'Great Old Ones' existed a hundred and fifty million years ago, and his idea had gained popular credence. This, of course, was inconceivable. Reich's neutron dater later suggested that the remains were less than two million years old, and even this may be an overestimate.

* See *Dalgleish Fuller, A Study in Fanaticism*, by Daniel Atherston. New York 2100.

The problems of dating are in this case unusually complex. The archaeologist usually relies on the various layers of earth above his find, for in these he possesses a kind of ready-made calendar. But in the three known cases of these giant cities, the clues seem contradictory. All that we can say with certainty is that each was destroyed by a deluge that buried them under many thousands of feet of mud. The word ' deluge ' immediately suggests the Pleistocene to a geologist – a mere million years ago. But in the Queensland deposits have been found traces of a rodent that is known to have existed only in the Pliocene era, which could add another five million years to the dating.

All this is irrelevant to my main story. For long before the completion of the first tunnel, I had lost interest in the Karatepe excavations. I had come to recognize them for what they were – a red herring deliberately introduced by the mind parasites.

My discovery came about in this way.

By the end of July 1997, I was in a state of total exhaustion. Even with a five mile sun-umbrella reducing the temperature to a mere sixty in the shade, Karatepe was intolerable. The rubbish dumped on us by Fuller's disciples made the place stink like a swamp; the various disinfectant fluids that were used to cover it up only made it worse. The winds were dry and dusty. We spent half the day drinking iced sherbert with rose leaves and reclining in the air-conditioned huts. In July, I began to get violent headaches. Two days spent in Scotland improved things, and I went back to work, but after another week, I went down with fever. I had had enough of constant interruptions from press men and Anti-Kadath cranks, so I went back to my flat in Diyarbakir. It was cool and quiet, being on the territory of the Anglo-Indian Uranium Company, whose guards had a short way with intruders. I found heaps of letters and several great parcels waiting for me, but for two days I ignored them, and stayed in bed and listened to the operas of Mozart on gramophone records. Gradually, the fever left me. On the third day, I had emerged from my accidie enough to open my letters.

Among them was a note from Standard Motors and Engineering, saying that, in accordance with my request, they were forwarding most of Karel Weissman's papers to me at Diyarbakir. This, then, explained the enormous parcels. Another letter came from Northwestern University Press, and enquired whether I would be willing to entrust them with the publication of Karel's psychological papers.

All this was tiresome. I forwarded the letter to Baumgart in London, and went back to my Mozart. The next day, conscience nagged me, and I opened the remainder of my post. And I found a letter from Carl Seidel, the man with whom Baumgart shared a flat (he was a homosexual) telling me that Baumgart had suffered a nervous breakdown, and was at present back with his family in Germany.

This obviously meant that the question of Karel's papers was now in my hands. So, with immense unwillingness, I went about the task of opening the first of the parcels. It weighed about forty pounds, and consisted entirely of the results of a test made upon a hundred employees to determine their response to colour changes. I shuddered, and turned back to *The Magic Flute*.

That evening, a young Persian executive with whom I had become friendly dropped in to share a bottle of wine. I was feeling a little lonely, and was glad to talk. Even the subject of the excavations had ceased to be unbearable to me, and it gave me pleasure to tell him the ' inside story' of our work. As he was leaving, he noticed the parcels, and asked if they were connected with the excavations. I told him the story of Weissman's suicide, and admitted that the idea of opening them produced a boredom that approached physical pain. In his cheerful and kindly way, he offered to return the next morning and open them for me. If they were all routine test papers, he would get his secretary to pack them straight off to Northwestern University. I knew he made the offer as a kind of repayment for my confidences of the evening, and I accepted cordially.

By the time I was out of my bath the next morning, he had finished. Five out of six parcels contained routine material. The sixth, he told me, seemed to be of a more 'philosophical nature', and he thought I might like to look at it. With that, he withdrew, and his secretary came shortly afterwards to remove the enormous pile of yellow foolscap pages from the middle of my sitting-room.

The remaining material was in neat blue folders, and consisted of typewritten pages held together by metal rings. The cover of each bore a handwritten label: *Historical Reflections*. Every folder was sealed with a coloured sticky tape, and I surmised – rightly, as it later turned out – that they had not been opened since Weissman's death. I never discovered what mistake had led Baumgart to send them to General Motors. I would guess that he put them by for my attention, and somehow packed them with the industrial material.

The folders were not numbered. I broke open the first, and quickly discovered that these 'historical reflections' covered only the history of the past two centuries – a period that had never held any great interest for me. I was tempted to send them off to Northwestern University without further examination, but conscience got the better of me. I retired to bed, and took the half-dozen blue folders with me.

This time, by accident, I started in the right place. The opening sentence of the first folder I opened read:

'It has been my conviction for several months now that the human race is being attacked by a sort of mind-cancer.'

An arresting sentence. I thought: Ah, what an excellent opening for a volume of Karel's papers ... A mind cancer, another name for neurosis or anhedonia, the spiritual malaise of the twentieth century ... Not for a moment did I take it literally. I read on. The strange problem of the rising suicide rate . . . The high incidence of child murder in the modern family . . . the perpetual danger of atomic war, the increase in drug addiction. It all seemed familiar enough. I yawned, and turned the page.

A few minutes later, I was reading with closer attention. Not because what I was reading struck me as true, but because I suddenly had a definite suspicion that Karel had gone insane. In my youth, I had read the books of Charles Fort, with their suggestions of giants, fairies and floating continents. But Fort's extraordinary farragos of sense and nonsense have an air of humorous exaggeration. Karel Weissman's ideas sounded as mad as Fort's, but they were obviously advanced in all seriousness. Either, then, he had joined the ranks of famous scientific eccentrics, or he had gone completely mad. In view of his suicide, I was inclined to the latter view.

I read on with a kind of morbid absorption. After the opening pages, he ceased to mention the ' mind cancer ', and launched into an examination of the cultural history of the past two hundred years . . . It was carefully argued, and brilliantly written. It revived memories of our long talks at Uppsala. At midday, I was still reading. And by one o'clock, I knew I had stumbled on something that would make me remember this day for the rest of my life. Mad or not, it was horribly convincing. I wanted to believe it was madness. But as I read on, my certainty was eroded. It was all so unsettling that I broke the habit of years, and drank a bottle of champagne at lunch time. As to food, it was all I could do to nibble a turkey sandwich. And despite the champagne, I became steadily more depressed and sober. And by late afternoon. I had grasped the whole tremendous and nightmarish picture, and my brain felt as if it would burst. If Karel Weissman was not insane, the human race confronted the greatest danger in its history.

It is obviously impossible to explain in detail how Karel

Weissman arrived at his 'philosophy of history'.* It was the result of a lifetime of work. But I can at least outline the conclusions he reached in his *Historical Reflections*.

The most remarkable faculty of mankind, says Weissman, is its power of self-renewal, or of creation. The simplest example is the kind of renewal that occurs when a man sleeps. A tired man is a man already in the grip of death and insanity. One of Weissman's most striking theories is his identification of insanity with sleep. A sane man is a man who is fully awake. As he grows tired, he loses his ability to rise above dreams and delusions, and life becomes steadily more chaotic.

Now Weissman argues that this faculty of creation or self-renewal is abundantly obvious in European man from the Renaissance to the eighteenth century. In this period, human history is full of cruelty and horror, and yet man can throw it off as easily as a tired child can sleep off its fatigue. The English Elizabethan period is usually cited as a golden age because of its creativity; but anyone who studies it closely is horrified by its callousness and brutality. Men are tortured and burnt alive; Jews have their ears cut off; children are beaten to death or allowed to die in incredibly filthy slums. Yet so enormous is man's optimism and power of self-renewal that the chaos only stimulates him to new efforts. Great age follows great age: the age of Leonardo, the age of Rabelais, the age of Chaucer, the age of Shakespeare, the age of Newton, the age of Johnson, the age of Mozart . . . Nothing is more obvious than that man is a god who will overcome every obstacle.

And then a strange change comes over the human race. It happens towards the end of the eighteenth century. The tremendous, bubbling creativity of Mozart is counterbalanced by the nightmare cruelty of De Sade. And suddenly, we are in an age of darkness, an age where men of genius no longer

* A detailed examination will be found in the three volumes of Max Viebig's *Philosophy of Karel Weissman*. Northwestern University, 2015.

create like gods. Instead, they struggle as if in the grip of an invisible octopus. The century of suicide begins. In fact, modern history begins, the age of defeat and neurosis.

But why did it all happen so *suddenly*? The industrial revolution? But the industrial revolution did not happen overnight, and neither did it affect a large area of Europe. Europe remained a land of woods and farms. How, asked Weissman, can we explain the immense difference between the genius of the eighteenth century and that of the nineteenth, except by surmising that some invisible yet cataclysmic change came over the human race in about the year 1800? How can the industrial revolution explain the total dissimilarity between Mozart and Beethoven – the latter a mere fourteen years Mozart's junior? Why do we enter a century in which half the men of genius committed suicide or died of tuberculosis? Spengler says that civilizations grow old like plants, but this is a sudden *leap* from youth to old age. An immense pessimism descends on the human race, which is reflected in its art, its music, its literature. It is not enough to say that man has suddenly grown up. What is far more important is that he seems to have *lost his power of self-renewal*. Can we think of a single great man of the eighteenth century who committed suicide? And yet their lives were just as hard as those of the nineteenth century. The new man has lost faith in life, he has lost faith in knowledge. Modern man agrees with Faust: that when all is said and done, we can know nothing.

Now Karel Weissman was a psychologist, not a historian. And the field in which he made a living was in industrial psychology. In the *Historical Reflections*, he writes:

It was in 1990 that I entered the field of industrial psychology as the assistant of Professor Ames at Trans-world Cosmetics. I immediately discovered a curious and nightmarish situation. I knew, of course, that ' industrial neurosis ' had become a serious matter – so much so that special industrial courts had been set up to deal with offenders who sabotaged machinery or killed or injured workmates. But only a few people were aware of the sheer size of the problem. The murder rate in large factories and similar concerns had increased to *twice* that of the rest of the population. In one cigarette factory in America, eight foremen and two high executives were killed in the course of a single year; in seven of these cases, the murderer committed suicide immediately after the attack.

The industrial Plastics Corporation of Iceland had decided to try the experiment of an ' open air ' factory, spread over many acres, so that the workers had no sense of overcrowding or confinement; energy fields were used instead of walls. At first, the experiment was highly successful; but within two years, the factory's rate of industrial crime and neurosis had risen to equal the national average.

These figures never reached the national press. Psychologists reasoned – correctly – that to publicize them would make things worse. They reasoned that it would be best to treat each case as one would an outbreak of fire that must be isolated.

The more I considered this problem, the more I felt that we had no real idea of its cause. My colleagues were frankly defeated by it, as Dr Ames admitted to me during my first week at Trans-world Cosmetics. He said that it was difficult to get to the root of the problem, because it seemed to have so many roots – the population explosion, overcrowding in cities, the individual's feeling of insignificance and increasing sense of living in a vacuum, the lack of adventure in modern life, collapse of religion . . . and so on. He said he wasn't sure that industry wasn't treating the problem in entirely the wrong way. It was spending more money on psychiatrists, on improving working conditions – in short, in making the workers feel like patients. But since our living depended on this mistake, it was hardly up to us to suggest a change.

And so I turned to history to find my answers. And the answers, when I found them, made me feel like suicide. For, according to history, all this was completely inevitable. Civilization was getting top heavy; it was bound to fall over. Yet the one thing this conclusion failed to take into account was the human power of self-renewal. By the same reasoning, Mozart was bound to commit suicide because his life was so miserable. But he didn't.

What was destroying the human power of self-renewal?

I cannot explain quite how I came to believe that there might be a *single cause*. It was something dawned on me slowly, over many years. It was simply that I came to feel increasingly strongly that the figures for industrial crime were out of all proportion to the so-called ' historical causes '. It was as if I were the head of a firm who begins to feel instinctively that his accountant is cooking the books, although he has no idea how it is being done.

And then, one day, I began to suspect the existence of the mind vampires. And from then on, everything confirmed my guess.

It happened first when I was considering the use of mescalin and lysergic acid for curing industrial neurosis. Fundamentally, of course, the effect of these drugs is no different from that of alcohol or tobacco: they have the effect of unwinding us. A man who is overworked has got himself into a habit of tension, and he cannot break the habit by merely willing. A glass of whisky or a cigarette will reach down into his motor levels and release the tension.

But man has far deeper habits than overwork. Through millions of years of evolution, he has developed all kinds of habits for survival. If any of these habits get out of control, the result is mental illness. For example, man has a habit of being prepared for enemies; but if he allows it to dominate his life, he becomes a paranoiac.

One of man's deepest habits is keeping alert for dangers and difficulties, refusing to allow himself to explore his own mind because he daren't take his eyes off the world around him. Another one, with the same cause, is his refusal to notice beauty, because he prefers to concentrate on practical problems. These habits are so deeply ingrained that alcohol and tobacco cannot reach them. But mescalin can. It can reach down to man's most atavistic levels, and release the automatic tensions that make him a slave to his own boredom and to the world around him.

Now I must confess that I was inclined to blame these

atavistic habits for the problem of the world suicide rate and the industrial crime rate. Man has to learn to relax, or he becomes overwrought and dangerous. He must learn to contact his own deepest levels in order to re-energize his consciousness. So it seemed to me that drugs of the mescalin group might provide the answer.

So far, the use of these drugs had been avoided in industrial psychology, for an obvious reason: mescalin relaxes a man to a point where work becomes impossible. He wants to do nothing but contemplate the beauty of the world and the mysteries of his own mind.

I felt that there was no reason to reach this limit. A tiny quantity of mescalin, administered in the right way, might release a man's creative forces without plunging him into a stupor. After all, man's ancestors of two thousand years ago were almost colour-blind because they were in a subconscious habit of ignoring colour. Life was so difficult and dangerous that they couldn't afford to notice it. Yet modern man has succeeded in losing this old habit of colour-blindness without losing any of his drive and vitality. It is all a matter of balance.

And so I inaugurated a series of experiments with drugs of the mescalin group. And my first results were so alarming that my engagement with Trans-world Cosmetics was terminated abruptly. Five out of my ten subjects committed suicide within days. Another two had a total mental collapse that drove them into a madhouse.

I was baffled. I had experimented with mescalin on myself in my university days, but I found the results uninteresting. A mescalin holiday is all very pleasant, but it all depends whether you enjoy holidays. I do not; I find work too interesting.

But my results made me decide to try it again. I took half a gram. The result was so horrifying that I still perspire when I think about it.

At first, there were the usual pleasant effects – areas of light swelling gently and revolving. Then an immense sense of peace and calm, a glimpse of the Buddhist nirvana, a beautiful and gentle contemplation of the universe that was at once detached and infinitely involved. After about an hour of this, I roused myself from it; I was obviously not discovering what had caused the suicides. Now I attempted to turn my attention *inward*, to observe the exact state of my perceptions and emotions. The result was baffling. It was as if I was trying to look through a telescope, and someone was deliberately placing his hand over the other end of it. Every attempt at self-observation failed. And then, with a kind of violent effort, I tried to batter through this wall of darkness. And suddenly, I had a distinct feeling of *something living and alien* hurrying out of my sight. I am not, of course, speaking of physical sight. This was entirely a 'feeling'. But it had such an imprint of reality that for a moment I became almost insane with terror. One can run away from an obvious physical menace, but there was no running away from this, because it was inside me.

For nearly a week afterwards, I was in a state of the most abject terror, and closer to insanity than I have ever been in my life. For although I was now back in the ordinary physical world, I had no feeling of safety. I felt that, in returning to everyday consciousness, I was like an ostrich burying its head in the sand. It only meant that I was unaware of the menace.

Luckily, I was not working at the time; it would have been impossible. And about a week later, I found myself thinking: Well, what are you afraid of? You've come to no harm. I immediately began to feel more cheerful. It was only a few days after this that Standard Motors and Engineering offered me the post of their chief medical officer. I accepted it, and plunged into the work of an enormous and complex organization. For a long time it left me no time for brooding or devising new experiments. And whenever my thoughts turned back to my mescalin experiments, I felt such a powerful revulsion that I always found some excuse for putting it off.

Six months ago, I finally returned to the problem, this time from a slightly different angle. My friend Rupert Haddon of Princeton told me of his highly successful experiments in rehabilitating sexual criminals with the use of L.S.D. In explaining his theories, he used a great deal of the terminology of the philosopher Husserl. It immediately became obvious to me that phenomenology is only another name for the kind of self-observation I had tried to carry out under mescalin, and that when Husserl talks about 'uncovering the structure of consciousness ', he only means descending into these realms of mental habit of which I have spoken. Husserl had realized that while we have ordnance survey maps that cover every inch of our earth, we have no atlas of our mental world.

Reading Husserl renewed my courage. The idea of trying mescalin again terrified me; but phenomenology starts from ordinary consciousness. So I again began making notes about the problems of man's inner world, and the geography of consciousness.

Almost at once, I became aware *that certain inner-forces* were resisting my researches. As soon as I began to brood on these problems, I began to experience sick headaches and feelings of nausea. Every morning, I woke up with a feeling of profound depression. I have always been a student of mathematics in an amateurish way, as well as a good chess player. I soon discovered that I felt better the moment I turned my attention to mathematics or chess. But the moment I began to think about the mind, the same depression would settle on me.

My own weakness began to infuriate me. I determined that I would overcome it at all costs. So I begged two months' leave of absence from my employers. I warned my wife that I was going to be very ill. And I deliberately turned my mind to these problems of phenomenology. The result was exactly as I predicted. For a few days I felt tired and depressed. Then I began to experience headaches and nerve pains. Then I vomited up everything I ate. I took to my bed, and tried to use my mind to probe my own sickness, using the methods of analysis laid down by Husserl. My wife had no idea of what was wrong with me, and her anxiety made it twice as bad. It is lucky that we have no children; otherwise, I would certainly have been forced to surrender.

After a fortnight, I was so exhausted that I could barely swallow a teaspoonful of milk. I made an immense effort to rally my forces, reaching down to my deepest instinctive levels. In that moment, I became aware of my enemies. It was like swimming down to the bottom of the sea and suddenly noticing that you are surrounded by sharks. I could not, of course, ' see ' them in the ordinary sense, but I could *feel* their presence as clearly as one can feel toothache. They were down there, at a level of my being where my consciousness never penetrates.

And as I tried to prevent myself from screaming with terror, the fear of a man facing inevitable destruction, I suddenly realized *that I had beaten them*. My own deepest life forces were rallying against them. An immense strength, that I had never known I possessed, reared up like a giant. It was far stronger than they were, and they had to retreat from it. I suddenly became aware of more of them, thousands of them; and yet I knew that they could do nothing against me.

And then the realization came to me with such searing force that I felt as if I had been struck by lightning. Everything was clear; *I knew everything*. I knew why it was so important to them that no one should suspect their existence. Man possesses more than enough power to destroy them all. But so long as he is unaware of them, they can feed on him, like vampires, sucking away his energy.

My wife came into the bedroom and was astounded to find me laughing like a madman. For a moment, she thought my mind had collapsed. Then she realized that it was the laughter of sanity.

I told her to go and bring me soup. And within forty-eight hours, I was back on my feet again, as healthy as ever – in fact, healthier than I had ever been in my life. At first, I felt such an immense euphoria at my discovery that I forgot about those vampires of the mind. Then I realized that this in itself was stupid. They had an immense advantage over me; they knew my own mind far better than I did. Unless I was very careful, they could still destroy me.

But for the moment, I was safe. When, later in the day, I felt the persistent, nagging attacks of depression, I turned again to that deep source of inner power, and to my optimism about the human future. Immediately the attacks ceased, and I began to roar with laughter again. It was many weeks before I could control this laughter mechanism whenever I had a skirmish with the parasites.

What I had discovered was, of course, so fantastic that it could not be grasped by the unprepared mind. In fact, it was extraordinary good luck that I had not made the discovery six years earlier, when I was working for Trans-world. In the meantime, my mind had made slow and unconscious preparation for it. In the past few months, I have become steadily more convinced that it was not entirely a matter of luck. I have a feeling that there are powerful forces working on the side of humanity, although I have no idea of their nature.

(I made a special note of this sentence. It was something I had always felt instinctively.)

What it amounts to is this. For more than two centuries now, the human mind has been constantly a prey to these energy vampires. In a few cases, the vampires have been able completely to take over a human mind and use it for their own purposes. For example, I am almost certain that De Sade was one of these ' zombis ' whose brain was entirely in the control of the vampires. The blasphemy and stupidity of his work are not, as in many cases, evidence of demonic vitality, and the proof of it is that De Sade never matured in any way, although he lived to be 74. The sole purpose of his life work is to add to the mental confusion of the human race, deliberately to distort and pervert the truth about sex.

As soon as I understood about the mind vampires, the history of the past two hundred years became absurdly clear. Until about 1780 (which is roughly the date when the first full-scale invasion of mind vampires landed on earth), most art tended to be life-enhancing, like the music of Haydn and Mozart. After the invasion of the mind vampires, this sunny optimism became almost impossible to the artist. The mind vampires always chose the most intelligent men as their instruments, because it is ultimately the intelligent men who have the greatest influence on the human race. Very few artists have been powerful enough to hurl them off, and such men have gained a new strength in doing so – Beethoven is clearly an example; Goethe another.

And this explains precisely why it is so important for the mind vampires to keep their presence unknown, to drain man's lifeblood without his being aware of it. A man who defeats the mind vampires becomes doubly dangerous to them, for his forces of self-renewal have conquered. In such cases, the vampires probably attempt to destroy him in another way – by trying to influence other people against him. We should remember that Beethoven's death came about because he left his sister's house after a rather curious quarrel, and drove several miles in an open cart in the rain. At all events, we notice that it is in the nineteenth century that the great artists first begin to complain that ' the world is against them '; Haydn and Mozart were well understood and appreciated by their own time. As soon as the artist dies, this neglect disappears – the mind vampires loosen their grip on people's minds. They have more important things to attend to.

In the history of art and literature since 1780, we see the results of the battle with the mind vampires. The artists who refused to preach a gospel of pessimism and life devaluation were destroyed. The life-slanderers often lived to a ripe old age. It is interesting, for example, to contrast the fate of the life-slanderer Schopenhauer with that of the life-affirmer Nietzsche, or that of the sexual degenerate De Sade with that of the sexual mystic Lawrence.

Apart from these obvious facts, I have not succeeded in learning a great deal about the mind vampires. I am inclined to suspect that, in small numbers, they have always been present on earth. Possibly the Christian idea of the devil arises from some obscure intuition of the part they had played in human history: how their role is to take over a man's mind, and to cause him to become an enemy of life and of the human race. But it would be a mistake to blame the vampires for all the misfortunes of the human race. Man is an animal who is trying to evolve into a god. Many of his problems are an inevitable result of this struggle.

I have a theory, which I will state here for the sake of completeness. I suspect that the universe is full of races like our own, struggling to evolve. In the early stages of its evolution, any race is mainly concerned to conquer its environment, to overcome enemies, to assure itself of food. But sooner or later, a point comes where the race has progressed beyond this stage, and can now turn its attention inward, to the pleasures of the mind. ' My mind to me a kingdom is ', said Sir Edward Dyer. And when man realizes that his mind is a kingdom in the most literal sense, a great unexplored country, he has crossed the borderline that divides the animal from the god.

Now I suspect that these mind vampires specialize in finding races who have almost reached this point of evolution, who are on the brink of achieving a new power, and then feeding on them until they have destroyed them. It is not their actual intention to destroy – because once they have done this, they are forced to seek another host. Their intention is to feed for as long as possible on the tremendous energies generated by the evolutionary struggle. Their purpose, therefore, is to prevent man from discovering the worlds inside himself, to keep his attention directed *outwards*. I think there can be no possible doubt that the wars of the twentieth century are a deliberate contrivance of these vampires. Hitler, like De Sade, was almost certainly another of their ' zombis '. A completely destructive world war would not serve their purposes, but continual minor skirmishes are admirable.

What would man be like if he could destroy these vampires, or drive them away? The first result would certainly be a tremendous sense of mental relief, a vanishing oppression, a surge of energy and optimism. In this first rush of energy, artistic masterpieces would be created by the dozen. Mankind would react like children who have been let out of school on the last day of term. Then man's energies would turn inward. He would take up the legacy of Husserl. (It is obviously significant that it was Hitler who was responsible for Husserl's death just as his work was on the brink of new achievements.) He would suddenly realize that he possesses inner-powers that make the hydrogen bomb seem a mere candle. Aided, perhaps, by such drugs as mescalin, he would become, for the first time, *an inhabitant of the world of mind*, just as he is at present an inhabitant of earth. He would explore the countries of the mind as Livingstone and Stanley explored Africa. He would discover that he has many ' selves ', and that his higher ' selves ' are what his ancestors would have called gods.

I have another theory, which is so absurd that I hardly dare to mention it. This is that the mind vampires are, without intending it, the instruments of some higher force. They may, of course, succeed in destroying any race that becomes their host. But if, by any chance, the race should become aware of

67

the danger, the result is bound to be the exact opposite of what is intended. One of the chief obstacles to human evolution is man's boredom and ignorance, his tendency to drift and allow tomorrow to take care of itself. In a certain sense, this is perhaps a greater danger to evolution – or at least, a hindrance – than the vampires themselves. Once a race becomes aware of these vampires, the battle is already half won. Once man has a purpose and a belief, he is almost invincible. The vampires might serve, therefore, to inoculate man against his own indifference and laziness. However, this is no more than a casual speculation . . .

The next problem is more important than all this speculation: How is it possible to get rid of them? It is no answer simply to publish ' the facts '. The historical facts mean nothing at all; they would be ignored. In some way, the human race has to be made aware of its danger. If I did what would be so easy – arranged to be interviewed on television, or wrote a series of newspaper articles on the subject – I might be listened to, but I think it more probable that people would simply dismiss me as insane. Yes, indeed, this is a tremendous problem. For short of persuading everyone to try a dose of mescalin, I can think of no way of convincing people. And then, there is no guarantee that mescalin would bring about the desired result – otherwise, I might risk dumping a large quantity of it in some city's water supply. No, such an idea is unthinkable. With the mind vampires massed for attack, sanity is too fragile a thing to risk. I now understand why my experiment at Transworld ended so disastrously. The vampires *deliberately destroyed* those people, as a kind of warning to me. The average person lacks the mental discipline to resist them. This is why the suicide rate is so high . . .

I *must* learn more about these creatures. While my ignorance is so complete, they could destroy me. When I know something about them, perhaps I shall also know how to make the human race aware of them.

The part of the statement I have quoted was not, of course, where I began; I have selected its central passage. The *Historical Reflections* were actually lengthy reflections on the nature of these mind parasites and on their part in human history. The work is in the form of a diary, a diary of ideas. Inevitably, it is extremely repetitive. He is a man who is trying to hold tight on to some central insight, and who keeps on losing it.

I was struck by the fact that he was able to concentrate for such long periods. Under his circumstances, I would certainly have found it harder to suppress my nervousness. But I came to believe that this was because he felt that he was now relatively safe from them. He had beaten them in the first battle, and he had the elation of victory. His main problem, as he said, was to get other people to believe him. Apparently, he did not consider this as too urgent. He knew that if he published his findings as they stood, he would be regarded as a madman. In any case, as a scientist, he had the habit of trying to verify his facts and to enlarge them as far as possible before announcing them. What puzzled me – and continues to puzzle me – is that he did not try to confide in anybody, not even in his wife. This in itself shows a peculiar state of mind. Was he so absolutely certain that he was now in no danger that he felt time no longer mattered? Or was this euphoria another trick of the parasites? Whatever happened, he went on working at his notes, convinced that he was fighting a winning battle – until the day they drove him to suicide.

I think my feelings as I read all this can be guessed. At first, incredulity – in fact, the incredulity kept returning all day; then excitement and fear. I think I might have dismissed the whole thing as insanity if it had not been for my experience on the wall at Karatepe. I was ready to believe in the existence of these mind vampires. But what then?

Unlike Weissman, I had not the strength to keep it to myself. I was terrified. I knew that the safest thing would be to burn the papers and pretend I had never read them; I was fairly sure that, in that case, they would leave me alone. I felt very close to insanity. All the time I was reading, I kept glancing around nervously, and then realizing that, if they were watching me, it was from *inside*. This was an almost unbearable thought until I came across the passage in which Weissman compares their method of 'eavesdropping' to listening over a radio. Then I saw that this was reasonable. They were apparently in the depth of consciousness, in the realm of the deepest memories. If they came too close to consciousness, they were in danger of revealing themselves. I came to the conclusion that they probably dared to come close to the surface late at night, when the mind was tired and attention was exhausted; this explained what had happened on the wall at Karatepe.

I already knew what would be my next move. I would have to tell Reich; he was the only man I liked and trusted deeply enough. Perhaps Karel Weissman's tragedy was that he liked and trusted no one as much as I liked and trusted Reich. But if I intended to tell Reich, then the safest time would be in the morning, when we were both wide awake. And I knew I was incapable of keeping this secret overnight.

And so I called Reich – on our private code – at the digging. As soon as his face appeared on the screen, I felt closer to sanity. I asked him if he felt like having a meal with me that evening. He asked me if I had any particular reason, and I said no – only that I was feeling better and felt like company. Luck was with me; some directors of A.I.U. were over there that afternoon and would be returning to Diyar-bakir by rocket at six o'clock. He would be with me by half past.

As I pulled out the plug, I had my first insight into why Weissman had kept silent about them. This idea of being 'overheard' – as if someone was tapping the telescreen line – led one to play safe, to behave calmly, to try to keep the thoughts restrained, running on common matters.

I ordered a meal downstairs in the director's restaurant, to which we had access. It seemed somehow safer to tell him there. And in the hour before his arrival, I lay back on the bed, my eyes closed, and deliberately tried to relax, to empty my mind.

The odd thing is that, by this time, it wasn't difficult. This exercise of concentrating upon one's own mind had an exhilarating effect. There were certain things that I began to understand immediately. As an unashamed 'romantic', I have always been subject to boredom. This boredom arises out of a kind of mistrust of the world. You feel you can't ignore it, can't take your eyes off it and forget it. So you sit staring at a corner of the ceiling when you could be listening to music or thinking about history, held by a strange sense of duty. Well, I now felt that my duty lay in ignoring the outside world. I knew what Karel meant: that it was vital for the parasites to keep us in ignorance of their existence. Merely to become aware of them was to gain a new feeling of strength and purpose.

Reich came sharp at half past six, and said I looked much better. We had a martini, and he told me what had been happening since I left the site – mostly squabbles about the best angle at which to sink the first tunnel. At seven o'clock, we went down to supper. They gave us a quiet table near the window, and several people nodded to us – we had both become international celebrities in the past two months. When we were seated at table, we ordered iced melon, and he reached for the wine list. I took it from him, saying: 'I don't want you to drink any more this evening. You'll see why later. We shall both need clear heads.'

He looked at me in astonishment.

'What's happening? I thought you said you had nothing on your mind?'

'I had to. What I've got to tell you has to be kept secret for the present.'

He said, smiling: 'If it's as bad as that, perhaps we'd better check the table for hidden microphones.'

I told him there was no need, because what I had to say

71

wouldn't be believed by an eavesdropper. He was looking baffled by this time, so I began by saying:

'Do I strike you as fairly normal and sane?'

'Of course you do!'

'And supposing I told you that in half an hour you'll be doubting my sanity?'

He said: 'For Christ's sake get on with it. I know you're not mad. What is all this about? Not some new idea about our underground city?'

I shook my head; and since he was looking bewildered by this time, I told him that I'd been reading Karel Weissman's papers all the afternoon. I said: 'I think I've discovered why he killed himself.'

'Why?'

'I think you'd better read this particular one yourself. He explains it better than I could. But the main point is this. I don't believe he was mad. It wasn't suicide – it was some kind of murder.'

All the time I was saying this, I was wondering if he would think *me* mad, and I tried to appear as calm and sane as possible. But it was a relief to see that nothing was further from his thoughts. He only said:

'Look, if you don't mind, we'll have a drink after all. I need one.'

So we ordered half a bottle of Nuits St Georges, and I helped him drink it. And I told him, as succinctly as I could, Weissman's theories about the mind parasites. I began by reminding him of my experience on the wall at Karatepe, and our discussion. Before I had finished speaking, my respect and liking for Reich had doubled. He would have been justified in humouring me and sending for a strait jacket as soon as he was out of my sight. And the brief account I gave him must have sounded insane enough. However, he realized that I had read something in Weissman's papers that had convinced me, and he was willing to be convinced himself.

As we went back upstairs after the meal, I remember my sense of unreality. If I was right, then the conversation that had just taken place was one of the most important in human history. Yet here we were, two ordinary human beings, trying to get back to the privacy of my room, and being accosted by fat, prosperous looking men who wanted us to meet their wives. It all seemed too normal and commonplace. I looked at the enormous bulk of Wolfgang Reich ambling ahead of me up the stairs, and wondered if he really believed the science fiction story I had told him. I knew that, to a large extent, my sanity depended on his believing me.

In my room, we drank orange juice. Reich now understood why I wanted to keep an absolutely clear head. He did not smoke. I handed him the folder of the *Historical Reflections*, and showed him the passage that I have printed above. I re-read it, seated beside him. When he had finished, he stood up and walked up and down the room without speaking. I said finally:

'You realize that, if this is not just a mad dream, I've placed your life in danger by telling you?'

He said: 'That doesn't bother me. It's been in danger before. But I'd like to know how far there is any real danger. I've not had your experience of these mind vampires, so I've no way of judging.'

'Neither have I. I know as little as you. Weissman's other volumes are full of speculations about them, but there's nothing definite. We have to start almost from scratch.'

He looked at me steadily for several moments, then said: 'You really believe this, don't you?'

I said: 'I wish I didn't.'

It was absurd; we were talking like two characters out of a Rider Haggard novel; yet it was all real. We talked to no purpose for half an hour or so, then he said:

'There's one thing that we have to do immediately, anyway. We must both make a tape recording about all this, and deposit it in a bank tonight. If anything happened to us in the night, it would serve as a warning. There's less chance of people thinking two of us are insane than one.'

He was right. We got out my tape recorder, and did what he suggested, reading extracts of Weissman's notes aloud. Reich had the last word. He said that he was not yet sure whether all this was madness or not. But it sounded sufficiently likely to justify this precaution. We still did not know how Weissman died, and we had his diary for the day before his suicide with notes that sounded completely sane.

When the tape was finished, we sealed it in a plastic box, and walked down to drop it into the night safe of the A.I.U.C. bank. Then I rang the manager at home, told him that we had deposited a tape containing certain important ideas in his night safe, and asked for it to be kept in his vault until it was needed. We encountered no difficulty here; he assumed that it was some important information that concerned the diggings and A.I.U., and promised to give it his personal attention.

I said I thought we now both needed a night's sleep, and explained my idea that the parasites have less power over the fully conscious mind. We agreed to keep an open telescreen line between us all night, in case either needed help. Then we separated. Without hesitation, I took a strong sedative – although it was barely ten o'clock – and went to bed. When my head touched the pillow, I willed myself not to lie awake and think, and I fell asleep immediately. My thoughts felt ordered and disciplined; I had no difficulty in preventing my mind from wandering.

At nine the next morning, Reich woke me up, and sounded relieved to find I was all right. Ten minutes later, he came over to have breakfast.

It was now, sitting in a sunlit room and drinking iced orange juice, that we did our first useful thinking about the parasites. Our minds felt alert and fresh, and we recorded the whole conversation on tape. First of all, we discussed the problem of how far we could keep our knowledge a secret from them. The answer was that we had no way of knowing. Yet Weissman had survived for six months, which indicated that the danger was not immediate. What is more, they *knew* that Weissman was on to them; they had actually resisted his attempts to turn his mind upon the problem. So he was a marked man from the beginning. On the other hand, I had felt no alien presences the day before as I read the *Historical Reflections*, and after I had mastered that initial feeling of anxiety and panic I had felt exceptionally healthy, mentally and physically. I was rising to the challenge. (My grandmother once told me that during the early days of the last World War, everyone seemed happier and more resilient than ever before, and now I understood perfectly.)

So it was possible that ' they ' didn't yet realize that Weissman's secret was out of the bag. This was hardly surprising. We did not know their numbers – or even whether the concept of number applied to them – but if they had the problem of policing five billion people – the present world population – then the danger was not too great. Let us, said Reich, suppose that Jung's theory is correct, and that the human race has one great ' mind ', a vast ocean of the ' subconscious '. We also suppose that these parasites are creatures that inhabit the depths of this ocean, and avoid coming too close to the surface for fear of detection. In that case, they might not discover what we know for years, provided we did not give ourselves away, as Weissman did, by alarming them.

That set a problem. On the previous evening, we had both felt that the best way to learn more about the parasites was to experiment with drugs that would enable us to explore our own minds. Now we realized that this would be dangerous. In that case, was there any way in which we could learn about the mind without the use of drugs?

Luckily for us, this was a problem about which Weissman had written at length. We discovered this in the course of the day, going through the *Reflections* page by page. Husserl's phenomenology was the method we needed. Husserl was concerned to map the 'structure of consciousness' (or its 'geography' as we preferred to say) by means of conscious reflection alone. And as we thought about the matter, we saw that this was common sense. If you are going to map an unknown continent – let us say, one of the jungles of Venus – you do not have to waste much time plodding among the trees. You rely mainly on instruments, and on your helicopter. What is most important is that you should become proficient at recognizing what is below you – knowing how to recognize swamp land by its colour, and so on. Well, where the geography of the human mind is concerned, the main problem is not to plunge into the realms below consciousness, but to learn to fit words to what we *do* know about it. With the use of a map, I could walk from Paris to Calcutta; without a map, I might find myself in Odessa. Well, if we had a similar 'map' of the human mind, a man could explore all the territory that lies between death and mystical vision, between catatonia and genius.

Let me put this another way. Man's mind is like some vast electronic brain, capable of the most extraordinary feats. And yet unfortunately, man does not know how to operate it. Every morning when he wakes up, man crosses to the control panel of that vast brain, and proceeds to turn knobs and press buttons. And yet this is the absurdity: with the immense machine at his disposal, he knows only how to make it do the simplest things, to deal with the most obvious, everyday problems. It is true that there are certain men whom we call men of genius, who can make it do far more exciting things: write symphonies and poems, discover mathematical laws. And then there are a few men who are perhaps the most important of all: men who use this machine *to explore its own capabilities*. They use the machine to find out what they can do with the machine. They know that it is capable of creating the Jupiter symphony and *Faust* and *The Critique of Pure Reason* and multi-dimensional geometry. Yet in a sense, these works have been achieved by accident, or, at least, by instinct. Well, many great scientific discoveries have been stumbled on by accident; but when they have been discovered, the scientist's first task is to learn the hidden laws that govern them. And this electronic brain is the greatest of all mysteries, for to know its secret would turn man into a god. So to what better purpose can consciousness be employed than to explore the laws of consciousness? And this is the meaning of the word ' phenomenology ', perhaps the most important single word in the vocabulary of the human race.

The sheer size of the task overawed us. Yet it did not depress us. No scientist could be depressed at the prospect of endless discovery. Again and again – I should say a thousand times over the next few months – we made the same remark : that we could understand the vampires' need for secrecy. Because everything depended on the human race taking its mental sickness for granted as a natural condition. Once it began to question it, to fight it, nothing could stand in its way.

I remember that we went down to the canteen for tea at mid-morning. (We decided that coffee might qualify as a drug, and should be avoided.) As we crossed the main square of A.I.U., we found ourselves looking at these people around us with a kind of god-like pity. They were all so preoccupied with their petty worries, all enmeshed in their personal little daydreams, while we at last were grappling with *reality* – the only true reality, that of the evolution of mind.

There was one immediate result. I began to lose my excess weight, and my physical health became perfect. I always slept well and deeply, and awoke feeling calm and totally healthy. My mental processes began to gain a feeling of amazing precision. I thought calmly, slowly, almost pedantically. We both realized the importance of this. Weissman had compared the parasites to sharks. Well, the quickest way for a swimmer to attract the attention of a shark is to splash and shout on the surface. We were not going to make that mistake.

Both of us returned to the diggings, but soon made excuses to spend a minimum of time there. This was not difficult, for most of what remained to be done was a problem for engineers rather than archaeologists. Reich, in any case, had thought of moving his equipment to Australia, to investigate the site described by Lovecraft in *The Shadow out of Time*, since our present finds left no doubt that Lovecraft was some sort of clairvoyant, and the possibility was worth exploring. Now, in August, we simply decided to take a holiday, making the hot season our excuse.

Both of us were daily on the lookout for any sign of the parasites. We were working well and smoothly; both of us were experiencing the same sense of physical and mental well-being, and we maintained a constant vigilance for any of the kind of mental ' interference ' that Karel had described. There was none, and we were puzzled about it. I accidentally discovered the reason when I revisited London in early October. The lease on my Percy Street flat needed renewing, and I could not make up my mind whether it was worth the trouble. So I took the morning rocket to London, and was in my flat by eleven in the morning. And the moment I entered, I knew they were watching me. Months of expecting them had sensitized me. In the old days, I would have ignored this sudden feeling of depression, of some obscure danger, dismissed it as indigestion. Since then, I had learned a great deal. I had learned, for example, that when human beings have that unheralded ' shivery ' feeling, which they describe as ' someone walking on my grave ', it is usually an alarm signal; some parasite has blundered too close to the surface of consciousness, and the shiver is due to awareness of the presence of the alien.

In my room, I knew immediately that the mind parasites were watching me. It may sound paradoxical to say that they were 'there' in my room, when I have already said they were *inside* me. This is due to the inadequacy of everyday language. In a certain sense, universal mind and universal space-time are coincidental, as Whitehead understood. Mind is not really 'inside' us in the same sense that our intestines are. Our individuality is a kind of eddy in the sea of mind, a reflection of the total identity of the universal humanity. So when I went into my room, the parasites were at once inside me and waiting for me there. It was the papers they were there to guard.

The weeks of training had had their effect. I allowed my mind to bend to the sway of their observation as a tree might bend in the wind, or as a sick man bends to his sickness. Again, I had a feeling of being observed by octopuses rather than sharks, by baleful creatures of stillness. I went about my business pretending not to notice them. I even went over to the cabinets and glanced inside, allowing the upper part of my mind to respond to the folders on psychology with its usual indifference. It was now that I became clearly aware that I had developed a new power of mind. I was quite detached from the human being I would have called 'Gilbert Austin' two months earlier, as detached as a puppet master from his puppet. And yet while I was being watched by the parasites, I blended into my old self, and became, so to speak, a mere passenger of my old self. I had no fear that I might give myself away. I was too well-controlled for that. I had switched over on to the circuits of the old 'Gilbert Austin', and it was now he who walked around the room, rang Hampstead to enquire after Mrs Weissman's health, and finally rang a storage firm to take away the furniture (which was my own) and the filing cabinets to a warehouse. After that, I went down and spoke to my landlord, then spent the rest of the day in the British Museum talking to Herman Bell, head of the archaeology department. All the time, I was still aware of being under the observation of the parasites, although more distantly now. Since I had told the removal firm to fetch the filing cabinets, their interest had obviously slackened.

For nearly forty-eight hours, I controlled my mind to think of nothing but routine matters connected with the Karatepe digging. This was not as difficult as it sounds (as many of my second stage readers will know.) It was merely a matter of identifying myself with my part, like a ' method actor ', of participating in Bell's excitement about the excavations, and so on. I walked around London and saw friends; I allowed myself to be lured to a ' small party ' to be lionized. (It turned out to be an enormous party; the hostess rang about a hundred guests as soon as I promised to be there.) I deliberately allowed my mind to work in its old manner: that is to say, badly. I let myself get over-excited, and then depressed. On the plane home, I allowed myself to wonder whether the whole thing had not been a stupid waste of time, and made a resolution not to let myself be lionized in this manner again. When the A.I.U. helicopter landed me in Diyarbakir, I had a feeling that the sky was clear again; but I continued to shield my thoughts for the next forty-eight hours, just in case. Reich was luckily back at the diggings, so there was no temptation to relax my precautions. As soon as he returned, I told him my story. I said I thought that the removal of the filing cabinets into storage probably reduced ' their ' interest in me to nil. But neither of us had any intention of allowing ourselves to become over-confident.

This experience led us to formulate another theory about the parasites. Clearly, they did not keep watch on every human being all the time. In that case, why did not people simply ' recover ', as we had, when there were no parasites around?

The question bothered us for twenty-four hours. It was Reich who came up with the answer. He happened to talk to the wife of Everett Reubke, the President of A.I.U.; her husband had just gone off for a fortnight to the moon as a ' rest cure '. She admitted that his nerves were ragged. ' But why?' asked Reich. Surely things were going excellently for the company? ' Oh yes,' she said. ' But when a man is President of a concern as big as A.I.U., he gets into the habit of worrying, and sometimes can't stop.'

That was it! Habit! How obvious, how self-evident, when you thought about it! Psychologists had been telling us for years that the human being is largely a machine. Lord Leicester compared human beings to grandfather clocks driven by watch springs. A single traumatic experience in childhood could be the foundation for a lifelong neurosis. One or two happy experiences in early childhood can make a man an optimist for life. The body will destroy the germs of a physical illness within a week; but the mind will preserve germs of morbidity or fear for a lifetime. Why? Because the mind tends to be stagnant, as far as the life-forces go. It works on habit, and these habits are tremendously difficult to break, particularly the negative ones.

In other words, once a human being has been ' conditioned ' by the mind parasites, he is like a clock that has been wound up; he only requires attention once every year or so. Besides, Weissman discovered, human beings ' condition ' one another, and save the parasites work. The parents' attitude to life is passed on to the children. One gloomy and pessimistic writer with a powerful style affects a whole generation of writers, who in turn affect almost every educated person in the country.

THE MORE we learned of the parasites, the more we realized how terrifyingly simple the whole thing was, and the more it seemed an impossible piece of luck that we should have stumbled on their secret. It was to be a very long time before we understood that ' luck ' is as unsatisfactory and vague as most of the abstract nouns in our language, and that something quite different was at issue.

Naturally, we spent a lot of time discussing who else could be entrusted with our secret. This was a difficult problem.

We had made a good start, but one false step could ruin everything. First of all, we had to make sure that we picked people who were mentally ready to receive what we had to say. This was not so much a matter of being thought insane – we were no longer very worried about that – but of making sure that some carelessly chosen 'ally' did not give the whole thing away.

We did much reading of psychology and philosophy, to find out whether there were other minds that were already thinking along the right lines. We found several, but we were still cautious. By luck, Reich and I had quickly picked up the techniques of phenomenology; because neither of us were philosophers, and had no preconceptions to get rid of, Husserl's seed fell on fertile ground. But since this was a battle, we had to work out a way of *training* people to this mental discipline. It was not enough to rely on their ordinary intelligence. They had to be taught to defend themselves against the mind parasites in the shortest possible space of time.

The fact, you see, is this. Once you have got the knack of using the mind properly, everything follows easily. It is a matter of breaking a habit that human beings have acquired over millions of years: of giving all their attention to the outside world, and thinking of 'imagination' as a kind of escapism, instead of recognizing that it is a brief excursion into the great unknown countries of the mind. You had to get used to thinking how your mind worked. Not just your 'mind' in the ordinary sense, but your feelings and perceptions as well. I found that by far the most difficult thing, to begin with, was to realize that 'feeling' is just another form of perception. We tend to keep them in separate compartments. I look at a man, and I 'see' him; that is objective. A child looks at him and says: 'Ooh, what a horrid man'. The child *feels* about him, and we say that is 'subjective'. We are unaware of how stupid these classifications are, and how much they confuse our thinking. In a sense, the child's feeling is also a 'perception'. But in a far more important sense, our 'seeing' is also a feeling.

Think for a moment of what happens if you are trying to adjust a pair of binoculars. You turn the little wheel, and everything is a blur. Suddenly, a single extra turn makes everything become clear and sharp. Now think what happens if someone says to you: 'Old So-and-so died last night'. Usually, your mind is so full of other things that you don't feel anything at all – or rather, your feeling is *indistinct*, blurred, just as if the binoculars are out of focus. Perhaps weeks later, you are sitting quietly in your room reading, when something reminds you of old So-and-so who died, and quite suddenly you feel acute grief for a moment. The feeling has come into focus. What more is necessary to convince us that feeling and perception are basically the same thing?

This is a work of history, not of philosophy, so I do not propose to go into phenomenology at any length. (I have done so in other books, and I would also suggest the books of Lord Leicester as an excellent introduction to the subject.) But this much philosophy is necessary to understand the history of the fight against the mind parasites. Because, as we realized when we thought about this matter, the chief weapon of the parasites was a kind of 'mind-jamming device' that could be loosely compared to a radar-jamming device. The conscious human mind 'scans' the universe all the time. 'The wakeful life of the ego is a perceiving'. It is like an astronomer scanning the skies for new planets. Now an astronomer discovers new planets by comparing old star photographs with new ones. If a star has moved, then it isn't a star, but a planet. And our minds and feelings are also constantly engaged in this process of scanning the universe for 'meanings'. A 'meaning' happens when we compare two lots of experience, and suddenly understand something about them both. To take an extremely simple example, a baby's first experience of fire may give it the impression that fire is wholly delightful: warm, bright, interesting. If he then tries putting his finger into the fire, he learns something new about it – that it burns. But he does not therefore decide that fire is wholly unpleasant – not unless he is exceptionally timid and neurotic. He superimposes the two experiences, one upon another, like two star maps, and marks down that one property of fire must be clearly separated from its others. This process is called learning.

Now supposing the mind parasites deliberately ' blur ' the feelings when we try to compare our two experiences. It would be as if they had exchanged an astronomer's spectacles for a pair with lenses made of smoked glass. He peers hard at his two star maps, but cannot make much out. We do not learn clearly from experience when this happens. And if we happen to be weak or neurotic, we learn entirely the wrong thing – that fire is ' bad ' because it burns, for example.

I apologize to non-philosophical readers for these explanations, but they are quite essential. The aim of the parasites was to prevent human beings from arriving at their maximum powers, and they did this by ' jamming ' the emotions, by blurring our feelings so that we failed to learn from them, and went around in a kind of mental fog. Now Weissman's *Historical Reflections* were an attempt to examine the history of the past two centuries to discover exactly how the parasites had conducted their attack on the human race. And this was one of the first things he realized. Take those ' romantic ' poets of the early nineteenth century – men like Wordsworth, Byron, Shelley, Goethe. They were quite different from the poets of the previous century – Dryden, Pope and the rest. Their minds were like powerful binoculars with a sharper power of focusing human existence. When Wordsworth looked down on the Thames from Westminster Bridge in the early morning, his mind suddenly roared like a dynamo, and superimposed a great many experiences on top of one another. For a moment, he saw human life from *above*, like an eagle, instead of from our

84

usual worm's eye view. And whenever a man sees life in this way – whether he is a poet or a scientist or a statesman – the result is a tremendous feeling of power and courage, a glimpse of what life is all about, of the meaning of human evolution.

Well, it was at this point in history, just as the human mind had taken this tremendous evolutionary leap forward – evolution always proceeds by leaps, like an electron jumping from one orbit to another – that the mind parasites struck in force. Their campaign was cunning and far sighted. They proceeded to manipulate the key minds of our planet. Tolstoy glimpsed this truth in *War and Peace*, when he declared that individuals play little part in history, that it moves mechanically. For all of the protagonists of that Napoleonic war *were* moving mechanically – mere chess men in the hands of the mind parasites. Scientists were encouraged to be dogmatic and materialistic. How? By giving them a deep feeling of psychological insecurity that made them grasp eagerly at the idea of science as ' purely objective ' knowledge – just as the parasites had tried to divert Weissman's mind into mathematical problems and chess. The artists and writers were also cunningly undermined. The parasites probably looked with horror upon giants like Beethoven, Goethe, Shelley, realizing that a few dozen of these would set man firmly on the next stage of his evolution. So Schumann and Hölderlin were driven mad; Hoffmann was driven to drink, Coleridge and De Quincey to drugs. Men of genius were ruthlessly destroyed like flies. No wonder the great artists of the nineteenth century felt that the world was against them. No wonder Nietzsche's brave effort to sound a trumpet call of optimism was dealt with so swiftly – by a lightning-stroke of madness. I shall not go into this matter at length now – Lord Leicester's books on the subject document it exhaustively.

Now, as I have said, the moment we recognized the existence of the mind parasites, we escaped their cunningly laid trap. For it was nothing less than a *history trap*. History itself was their chief weapon. They 'fixed' history. And in two centuries, human history became a parable of the weakness of human beings, the indifference of nature, the helplessness of man confronting Necessity. Well, the moment we knew that history had been 'fixed', it ceased to take us in. We looked back on Mozart and Beethoven and Goethe and Shelley, and thought: Yes, great men would have been two a penny if it hadn't been for the parasites. We saw that it is nonsense to talk about human weakness. Human beings have enormous strength when it is not being sucked away every night by these vampire bats of the soul.

This knowledge in itself was naturally enough to fill us with enormous optimism. And at this early stage, this optimism was increased by our ignorance of the parasites. Since we knew that they attached such importance to secrecy, to the human race being ignorant of their existence, we leapt to the conclusion – for which we would pay dearly – that they had no real power of doing harm. The problem of Karel's suicide bothered us, but his widow had provided me with a plausible theory. Karel took saccharines in his tea. The bottle of cyanide tablets resembled the saccharine bottle. Supposing he was working hard, and had absent-mindedly dropped cyanide in his tea instead of saccharine? The smell would give it away, of course. But supposing the parasites had some way of blanketing the sense of smell, 'jamming' it, so to speak? Perhaps Karel was sitting unsuspecting at his desk, concentrating upon his work, rather over-tired, perhaps. He reaches out automatically for the saccharine, and one of the parasites gently guides his hand a few inches to the left . . .

Reich and I were both inclined to accept this theory, which fitted with the presence of cyanide in the tea. It also fitted with our view that the parasites were fundamentally no more dangerous than any other parasite – woodworm or poison ivy – that, provided you knew about them and took meas-

86

ures against them, all would be well. We told ourselves that we would not be as vulnerable as Karel Weissman. There were a limited number of ways in which the parasites could try to trick us as they had tricked Karel. They might lead us to make some error when driving a car, for example. Driving is very much a matter of instinct, and this instinct could easily be tampered with when you were driving at ninety miles an hour and concentrating on the road. So we agreed never to drive in a car, under any circumstances, or to allow ourselves to be driven. (A chauffeur would be even more vulnerable than we ourselves.) Travelling by helicopter was another matter – the automatic radar controls meant that a crash was almost impossible. And one day, when we heard that a soldier had been killed by a berserk native, we realized that this was another possibility that had to be taken into account. For that reason, both of us carried guns, and made a point of avoiding crowds.

Still, during those first months, everything went so well that it was difficult not to become over-optimistic. In my early twenties, when I was learning about archaeology under Sir Charles Myers, I experienced a delight, an intensity, that made me feel I had only just started living. But it was nothing to the intensity that I now felt continuously. It became clear that there is a fundamental *mistake* about ordinary human existence – as absurd as trying to fill a bath with the plug out, or driving a car with the hand brake on. Something that ought to build up into a greater and greater intensity is lost minute by minute. Once this is recognized, the problem vanishes. The mind begins to brim with a sense of vitality and control. Instead of being at the mercy of moods and feelings, we control them as easily as we control the movements of our hands. The result can hardly be described to anyone who has not experienced it. Human beings get so used to things 'happening' to them. They catch cold; they feel depressed; they pick something up and drop it; they experience boredom . . . But once I had turned my attention into my own mind, these things ceased to happen, because I now controlled them.

I can still remember the greatest experience of those early days. I was sitting in the library at A.I.U. at three o'clock one afternoon, reading a new paper on linguistic psychology, and speculating whether its author could be trusted with our secret. Some references to Heidegger, the founder of this school, excited me, for I suddenly saw clearly the error that had crept into the foundation of his philosophy, and how, with this error corrected, tremendous new prospects would open up. I started to make shorthand notes. At this moment, a mosquito buzzed viciously past my ear with its high pitched whine; a moment later, it came past again. My mind still full of Heidegger, I glanced up at it, and wished that it would find its way to the window. As I did so, I had a distinct sense of my mind *encountering* the mosquito. It veered suddenly off its course and buzzed across the room to a closed window. My mind kept a firm grasp on it, and steered it across the room to the fan vent in the open window, and outside.

I was so astonished that I sat back and gaped after it. I could hardly have been more astonished if I had suddenly sprouted wings and started to fly. Had I been deceived in supposing that my mind had *guided* the creature? I remembered that the washroom had a plague of wasps and bees, for there was a bed of peonies underneath its window. I went along there. It was empty, and there was a wasp buzzing against the frosted glass of the window. I leaned my back against the door, and concentrated on it. Nothing happened. It was frustrating – there was a sense of doing something wrong, like trying to pull open a locked door. I cast my mind back to Heidegger, felt the lift of exaltation, of vision, and suddenly felt my mind *click into gear*. I was in contact with the wasp, just as certainly as if I was holding it in my hand. I willed it to move across the room. No, 'willed it' is the wrong phrase. You do not 'will' your hand to open and close; you just do it. In the same way, I drew the wasp across the washroom towards me; then, just before it reached me, made it turn and veer back to the window, and out. It was so incredible that I could have burst into tears, or roared with laughter. What made it so funny was that I could somehow feel the wasp's angry astonishment at being made to do this against its will.

Another wasp buzzed in – or perhaps the same one. I caught it again. This time, I was aware of my fatigue. My mind wasn't used to this kind of thing, and its grip was slipping. I went to the window and looked out of the flap at the top. A large bumble bee was rifling the honey from a peony. I let my mind grasp it, and willed it to come out. It resisted, and I could feel its resistance as directly as one can feel the pull of a dog on its lead when you take it for a walk. I exerted my strength, and it buzzed angrily out of the flower. I suddenly felt mentally tired, and let it go. However, I did not do what I used to do in the old stupid days – let my fatigue plunge me into depression. I simply let my mind relax, deliberately soothing it, and turned my thoughts elsewhere. Ten minutes later, in the library, the feeling of mental cramp had disappeared.

I now wondered whether I could exercise this same mental power over dead matter. I turned my attention to a lipstick-stained cigarette butt that someone had left in an ashtray at the next table, and tried to move it. Yes, it switched across the ashtray, but it cost me a far greater effort than with the bee. And at the same time I received another surprise. I felt a distinct shock of sexual desire in my loins as my mind touched the cigarette. I withdrew from it, then touched it again; once again I felt the shock. I discovered later that the cigarette butt had belonged to the secretary of one of the directors, a full-lipped, dark-haired woman who wore very powerful hornrimmed glasses. She was about thirty-five, unmarried, rather neurotic, and neither attractive nor unattractive. At first, I assumed that the shock of desire had come from me – had been a normal male reaction to the sexual stimulus of the lipstick-stained cigarette. But next time she came to sit near me in the library, I let my mind reach out cautiously to touch her, and was almost electrocuted by the musky, animal shock of sexual desire that came from her. It was not that she was actually thinking about sex – she was wading through a volume of statistics – or that she felt desire for any particular person. She apparently lived with this high-tension sexual current, and regarded it as perfectly normal.

I learned something else from her. As my mind withdrew from the contact, she glanced at me speculatively. I went on reading, and pretended not to notice her. After a while, she lost interest and went back to her statistics. But it proved that she had been aware of my ' mental probe'. The men I had tried it on had remained totally unaware. It seemed to prove that a woman, particularly a sexually frustrated woman, has an abnormal sensitivity to such things.

However, this came later. For the moment, I only tried moving the cigarette butt, and found that, although it could be done, it was hard work. This was because it was dead. It is easier to make a living object do what you want, because its vitality can be used by you, and there is no inertia to overcome.

Later that afternoon, still absorbed in my new discovery, I tore up some cigarette paper into tiny pieces, and amused myself by making the small flock rush around the table like a snowstorm. This was also exhausting, and I had to give it up after about fifteen seconds.

That evening, Reich came over from Karatepe, and I told him of my discovery. He was even more excited than I was. Oddly enough, he did not immediately try the experiment himself. Instead, he analysed it and discussed its possibilities. Of course, human beings had known about this possibility of ' psychokinesis' for half a century, and Rhine had investigated it at Duke. He defined psychokinesis (or PK) as a phenomenon ' in which the individual produces an effect

90

upon some object in his environment without the use of his own motor system '. ' Thus ', he adds, ' psychokinesis is the direct action of mind upon matter '. Rhine had been put on to the problem by a gambler who remarked that many gamblers believe they can influence the fall of the dice. He conducted thousands of experiments into the matter, and his results revealed what I had myself experienced – that, after a while, the mind gets tired of exercising ' psychokinesis '. There were far more ' hits ' at the beginning of the experiment than later on, and the number reduced steadily as the experiment proceeded.

So human beings have always possessed PK powers in a minor degree. The increase in strength of my mind since I had been practising phenomenological disciplines simply meant that I was able to direct a more powerful stream of mental energy into psychokinesis.

Reich's mind soared like a hawk released from its lead. He predicted the day when we would be able to raise the ruins of Kadath to the surface with no machinery of any sort, and when man would be able to travel to Mars by a spontaneous act of will, without the need for a space ship. His excitement infected me, for I saw that he was correct in saying that this was our greatest advance so far, in a philosophical as well as a practical sense. For, in a certain sense, man's scientific progress has been progress in the wrong direction. Take the matter of the Karatepe diggings; we had been treating it purely as a mechanical problem, how to raise a city from underneath a billion tons of earth, and this reliance on machines meant that we were ceasing to treat *the human mind* as an essential element in the operation. And the more this same human mind produces labour-saving machines, the more it blinds itself to its own possibilities, the more it tends to regard itself as a passive ' reasoning machine '. Man's scientific achievement over the past centuries had only thrust man deeper and deeper into a view of himself as a passive creature.

I warned Reich that so much mental excitement might attract the attention of the parasites. At this, he forced himself to be calm. I tore up a few cigarette papers, and moved them across the desk for him, pointing out as I did so that it was all I could do to move these two grammes of paper – so that, in fact, I was better equipped to dig my way to the ruins of Kadath with a pick and shovel than with my mind! Reich now tried moving the papers, and failed. I tried to explain to him the ' trick ' of getting the mind into gear, but he couldn't do it. He tried for half an hour, and couldn't move even the tiniest piece of paper. He finished the evening more depressed than I had seen him for a long time. I tried to cheer him up by pointing out that it was simply a knack that might come at any moment. My brother could swim when he was three years old, but it took me until I was eleven to acquire the knack.

And, in fact, Reich acquired it about a week later. He rang me up in the middle of the night to tell me about it. He had been sitting up in bed reading a book on child psychology when it happened. Thinking about the way that some children seem to be ' accident prone ', he had recognized how far this is due to the child's own mind. And as he thought about these hidden mental forces that we learn to control with such painful effort, he suddenly realized that, in exactly the same way as an 'accident prone ' child, he had been holding back his own powers of psychokinesis. He concentrated on the page of his book – which was of India paper – and made it turn of its own accord.

I gathered from him the next day that he had not bothered to sleep; he had simply spent the night practising PK. He discovered that the ideal material for these exercises was the ashes of burnt cigarette papers. These are so light that the slightest effort of the mind can move them. Moreover, the slightest puff of breath will send them spinning, and the mind can catch them in motion and utilize their energy.

After that, Reich developed his PK powers far more

quickly than I did, having a more powerful brain, as far as simple cerebral discharge is concerned. Within a week, I saw him perform the incredible feat of causing a bird to veer in its flight, and circle twice around his head. This act produced rather amusing consequences, for some secretaries saw him from a window, and one of them later told the press about it. When a reporter asked Reich about this ' omen ' of a black eagle circling his head (the story had grown in the telling), he had to declare that his family had always been bird lovers, and that he had used a special high pitched whistle to attract it. During the next month or so, his secretary had a full time job answering letters from societies of bird watchers who wanted him to come and lecture. After this, Reich took care to practise PK in the privacy of his room!

The fact is that I was not greatly interested in my powers of psychokinesis at this stage, for I failed to grasp their implications. It cost me such an effort to transport a sheet of paper across the room by PK that it was easier to get up and fetch it. So when I read the last act of Shaw's *Back to Methuselah*, in which his ' ancients ' can grow themselves extra arms and legs merely by willing, I felt that Shaw had passed well beyond the bounds of possibility.

The business of mapping these mental realms was in every way more exciting and rewarding, for it brought a far more exciting kind of control. Human beings are so used to their mental limitations that they take them for granted. They are like sick men who have forgotten the meaning of health. My mind could now command prospects that were beyond anything I had dreamed of before. For example, I had always been bad at mathematics. Now, without the slightest effort, I grasped the theory of functions, multi-dimensional geometry, quantum mechanics, game theory or group theory. I also read through the fifty volumes of the composite Bourabaki for bedtime reading – I found that I could skip whole pages at a time because the reasoning seemed so obvious.

I found that the mathematical studies were valuable in

many ways. If I turned my mind to my old love, history, it became so easy to ' realize ' a period, to grasp all its details with an imaginative intensity that made it into a reality, that I found it too exciting to bear. My mind would soar to a pitch of exalted contemplation that was only too likely to attract the attention of the parasites. So I stuck to mathematics, a safer study. Here my mind could turn intellectual somersaults, hurtle like a bullet from one end of the mathematical universe to the other, and still remain emotionally sober.

Reich was interested enough in my experience with the secretary at the next table to carry out some experiments in this direction. He discovered that about fifty per cent of the women, and thirty-five per cent of the men at A.I.U. were ' sexually overcharged '. This undoubtedly had something to do with the heat, and with poor domestic facilities. Now one might have expected that this intensity of sexual emotion would mean that A.I.U. would have a low industrial suicide rate. In fact, it had an exceptionally high one. And when Reich and I discussed this, we saw the reason. The sexual intensity and the high suicide rate were directly related – and related, of course, to the activity of the parasites. Sex is one of man's deepest sources of satisfaction; the sexual urge and the evolutionary urge are closely connected. Frustrate this deep urge in some way, and it overflows; it tries to find satisfaction in all kinds of basically unsatisfactory ways. One of these is promiscuity – of which there was a great deal at A.I.U. It is once again a matter of ' focusing ' emotion. A man believes that a particular woman will afford sexual satisfaction, and persuades her to become his mistress; but the parasites interfere, and he is unable to ' focus ' his energies in the sexual act. He is now rather bewildered. She has ' given ' herself, according to the common meaning of the phrase, and yet he remains unsatisfied. It is as baffling as eating a large meal and finding your hunger unsatisfied by it. There are two possible outcomes. He decides that the

94

trouble lies in his choice of woman, and promptly looks around for someone else. Or he decides that the ordinary sexual act is unsatisfying, and tries to devise ways of making it more interesting: that is to say, he explores the sexual perversions. Reich discovered, by a little discreet questioning, that a great many of the unmarried executives at A.I.U. had a reputation for ' peculiar ' sexual tastes.

A week after we had started discussing these sexual matters, Reich came into my room one night with a book, which he threw on my table.

' I've found a man we can trust.'

' Who? ' I snatched up the book and looked at its title. *Theories of the Sexual Impulse*, by Sigmund Fleishman, of the University of Berlin. Reich read passages aloud to me, and I saw what he meant. There could be no possible doubt that Fleishman was a man of exceptional intelligence who was baffled by the anomalies of the sexual impulse. But again and again he used phrases that sounded as if he suspected the existence of the mind parasites. He had recognized that sexual perversion is the result of some kind of polluting of man's sexual springs, and that there is an element of absurdity about it, like drinking whisky to quench your thirst. But why, he asked, should man in the modern world find sexual satisfaction so elusive? It is true that he tends to be sexually over-stimulated by books, magazines, films. But the urge to propagate the race is so strong that this should not make a great deal of difference. Even women, whose main instinct has always been to marry and raise children, seem to be succumbing to this rising tide of sexual abnormality and the number of divorce cases in which the husband accuses the wife of infidelity has been rising rapidly ... How can we explain this weakening of the evolutionary impulse in both sexes? Could there be some unknown factor, either physical or psychological, that we have failed to take into account?

As Reich commented, there were actually places in the book that sounded as if the author was blaming God for a piece of bungling in creating the human sexual impulse, and making it dependent on a sort of mutual frustration.

Yes, it was very obvious that Fleishman was our man, and that in this particular field, we might find others who were struck by the anomalies in the sexual impulse. One of our problems, of course, was how actually to contact the various possible allies – neither of us had time to rush around the world seeking out such people – but in this case it was made unexpectedly easy. I wrote to Fleishman, discussing certain points in his book, and professing an interest in the whole subject. I said vaguely that I might soon be taking a trip to Berlin, and would hope to call on him. Within a week, I received a long reply from him, in the course of which he said: 'Like everyone else in the world, I have been following your investigations with bated breath. Would you think me rude if I suggested coming to see you?' I replied telling him that he would be welcome at any time, and suggesting that very week-end. He sent me a telegram of acceptance. Three days later, Reich and I met him off the plane, at Ankara, and brought him back to Diyarbakir in the firm's rocket. Everything about him pleased us. He was a lively, intelligent man in his mid-fifties with a delightful sense of humour, and the typical German breadth of cultural interest. He could talk brilliantly about music, primitive art, philosophy and archaeology. He struck me as one of those few men who have a natural resistance to the mind parasites.

We gave him a good lunch at Diyarbakir, during which time we talked of nothing but the diggings and the problem posed by the ruins. In the afternoon, we flew out to Karatepe by rocket. (A.I.U. found our presence there such excellent publicity that we were allowed privileges that would have been unthinkable when Reich was only their consultant geologist.) The first tunnel was almost completed. We showed Fleishman what there was to see of it, then the rest of the 'exhibits' – the corner broken off the Abhoth block, the electronic photographs of the inscriptions on other blocks, and so on. He was fascinated by the whole problem – of a civilization older than the remains of Pekin Man. His own theory was interesting and plausible enough: it was that the earth had once been the site of an attempted settlement from another planet, probably Jupiter or Saturn. He agreed with Schrader's theory that all the planets had held life at some time. and probably – as we know in the case of Mars – intelligent life. He ruled out Mars because the size of the planet – its mass is a tenth of ours – and its low gravity ruled out the possibility of 'giants'; Jupiter and Saturn both have sufficient mass – and gravitation pull – to produce 'giants'.

Reich countered with his own theory: that the total population of earth had been destroyed several times through catastrophes involving the moon, and that after each destruction, man had painfully to evolve once again from earlier stages. If, as seems almost certain, these moon catastrophes involved great floods, it would explain why these ancient civilizations – millions of years older than Holocene man – were buried so deeply.

So the day passed by in wide-ranging discussions. In the evening, we went to see an excellent performance of *The Pirates of Penzance* by the A.I.U. operatic society, then had a leisurely meal in the director's restaurant. Reich had arranged for a bed to be made up in his own sitting-room, and it was there that we now went. But still we avoided the actual subject of the mind parasites, remembering the danger of discussing them late at night. But we *did* persuade Fleishman to talk at length about his theory of the sexual impulse. By midnight he was well into his stride, and had put before us a brilliant exposition of the whole problem. Sometimes we pretended to misunderstand him, forcing him to be more explicit. The results were rewarding beyond our hopes. Fleishman, with his sweeping scientific intelligence, had grasped the whole problem. He saw that man's sexual impulse is basically *romantic,* just like his poetic impulse. When a poet receives ' intimations of immortality ' from the sight of mountains, he knows perfectly well that the mountains are not really ' cloud-capped gods '. He knows that his own mind is *adding* their majesty to them – or rather, is seeing them as a symbol of the hidden majesty of his own mind. Their greatness and aloofness remind him of his own greatness and aloofness. And when a man falls romantically in love with a woman, again it is the poet in him that sees her as an instrument of evolution. The sheer power of the sexual impulse is the power of the god-like in man, and a sexual stimulus can arouse this power as a mountain can arouse his perception of beauty. We must see man, said Fleishman, not as a unity, but as a constant struggle between his higher and lower selves. Sexual perversion, as found in De Sade. represents these two locked together in conflict – locked together so tightly that you cannot prise them apart. It is the lower self deliberately using the energy of the higher self for its own purposes.

At this point, Reich interrupted. How, in that case, do you account for the steep rise in sexual perversion in this century?

Ah, precisely, Fleishman said gloomily. Man's lower self seems to be getting artificial support from somewhere. Perhaps our civilization is decadent, tired out, and its ' higher ' impulses are exhausted. Yet no, he could not believe that. Neither could he believe that the modern neurosis is due to man's inability to get used to being a civilized animal – in fact, a highly industrialized animal. Man has had plenty of time to get adjusted to big cities. No, surely the explanation must lie elsewhere . . .

At this point, I yawned, and said that I would like to continue the discussion over breakfast, if they wouldn't mind. We had a long and interesting day planned for Fleishman . . . Reich agreed with me. All this was too fascinating to discuss when we were tired. So we said goodnight, and all retired.

Next morning, at breakfast, we were glad to see that Fleishman was in sparkling spirits. He was obviously finding his week-end highly stimulating. When he asked us what we had planned for the day, we told him that it was something we would prefer to discuss after breakfast. Then we went back to Reich's room, and Reich continued the discussion exactly where we had broken off the night before. Reich quoted back Fleishman's remark: 'Man's lower self seems to be getting artificial support from somewhere'. Then he left it to me to tell the story of Karel Weissman, and our discovery of the parasites.

It took two hours, and we knew from the beginning that Fleishman had been an excellent choice. For perhaps twenty minutes he suspected an elaborate hoax. Karel's diaries convinced him otherwise. From then on, we saw the light breaking on him. When his excitement mounted, Reich quickly warned him that this was the most certain method of warning the parasites, and explained why we had waited until morning before telling him. Fleishman saw our point. From then on he listened quietly and seriously, and from the set of the lines of his mouth, it was clear that the parasites had found another formidable enemy.

In a way, Fleishman was easier to convince than Reich had been. To begin with, he had studied philosophy at college, and had done a term on Wilson and Husserl. And then, our PK demonstrations were particularly convincing. Fleishman had bought a ball made of coloured leather to take back for his granddaughter; Reich made this bounce all round the room. I exerted my powers and made a book float across the room, as well as holding a wasp buzzing angrily on the table, unable to move. As we went on explaining, Fleishman kept saying: 'My God, it all fits in.' One of the central concepts of his psychology is what he calls 'the tax on consciousness'. We were able to show him that this 'tax' is mostly imposed by the mind parasites.

99

Fleishman was our first pupil. We spent the whole day trying to teach him all we knew: how to sense the presence of the parasites, how to close the mind to them when they seem to be present. More than that was not necessary. He saw the main implication immediately: that by a kind of trick, man has been prevented from taking possession of a territory that belongs to him by right: the country of the mind; and that once an individual *knows* this with complete certainty, there is nothing whatever to prevent him from claiming his right. The veil of fog lifts, and man becomes a traveller in the mind as he has become a traveller on sea and in the air and in space. What he then does is up to himself. He can simply make brief pleasure trips into this new land, or he can set out to map it. We explained why, at present, we dared not use psychedelic drugs, and we told him of what we had been able to add to the realms of phenomenology.

We ate a large lunch – the morning's work had made us all ravenous – and afterwards it was Fleishman's turn to talk. As a psychologist, he knew many who had asked the same questions as himself. There were two more in Berlin: Alvin Curtis, of the Hirschfeld Institute, and Vincent Gioberti, one of his own ex-students, now a professor at the university. He told us of Ames and Thomson in New York, and Spencefield and Alexey Remizov at Yale, of Shlaf, Herzog, Klebnikov and Didring at the Massachusetts Institute. It was also at this point that he mentioned the name of Georges Ribot, the man who would almost destroy us . . .

It was also during the course of that afternoon that we first heard the name of Felix Hazard. Reich and I knew little about modern literature, but Hazard's sexual preoccupations had naturally interested Fleishman. We learned that Hazard had a high reputation among the *avant garde* for his curious blend of sadism, science fiction and world-weary pessimism. He was apparently paid a regular sum by a Berlin nightclub that catered for perverts, simply to come and sit there for a stated number of hours every month and be admired by the clientele. Fleishman described some of Hazard's work to us, and added the interesting information that he had begun life as a drug addict, but now claimed to have cured himself. Everything he told us about Hazard seemed to indicate that this man was another ' zombi ' of the mind parasites. Fleishman had met him only once, and had found it an unpleasant experience. He said that he had written in his diary: ' Hazard's mind is like a newly opened grave ', and that he had been strangely depressed for days after meeting him.

The question now arose: should we work closely together, or should we leave Fleishman to use his own discretion about making allies? We agreed that this latter might be a dangerous course: it would be better if all three of us could make such decisions together. On the other hand, there might be less time than we thought. The important thing was to gather a small army of men of high intellectual standing. Every one we added to our ranks made the task easier. Fleishman had been easy to convince because there were two of us. When there were enough of us, the whole world should be easy to convince. And then the real battle would commence . . .

In the light of what happened, it seems incredible that we could have been so confident. But it must be remembered that luck had been with us all the way, so far. And we had come to believe that the parasites were helpless against men who knew of their existence.

As we took Fleishman to his plane that evening, I remember him looking at the crowds in the brilliantly lit streets of Ankara, and saying: ' I feel as if I'd died over the week-end and been born a different person . . .' And in the air terminal, he remarked: 'It's strange, but all these people strike me as being *asleep*. They're all somnambulists.' We knew then that we had nothing to worry about where Fleishman was concerned. He was already taking possession of the ' country of the mind '.

And now things began to happen so swiftly that whole weeks seem a blur of events. Three days later, Fleishman was back to see us with Alvin Curtis and Vincent Gioberti. He arrived on Thursday morning, and left at five o'clock on Thursday evening. Curtis and Gioberti were all we could have wished, particularly Curtis, who seemed to have approached the problem through the study of existential philosophy, and who had come very close to suspecting the existence of the parasites through his own researches. Only one thing disturbed us. Curtis also mentioned Felix Hazard, and strengthened our suspicion that Hazard could be a *direct* agent of the parasites, a ' zombi ' whose mind had been completely taken over when he was in a drug-stupor. Apparently Hazard produced on many people a curious effect of evil, which neurotic young girls found stimulating. On Curtis, he had produced the same disturbing effect as on Fleishman. But what was worse, Hazard had twice sneered at Curtis's work in an *avant garde* magazine published in Berlin. Curtis had to be more careful than the rest of us; he was already suspect in the eyes of the parasites.

If we had not been fools, we would have arranged to have Hazard killed. It would not have been difficult. Fleishman had already developed rudimentary PK powers, and a little more training would strengthen them to a point where he could steer Hazard under a passing car – driven by Curtis or Gioberti. As it was, we felt the usual compunction. It was hard to realize that Hazard was *already* dead and that it was only a question of making his body useless to the parasites.

During the next three weeks, Fleishman came every weekend, always bringing a new ally with him – Spencefield, Ames, Cassell, Remizov, Lascaratos (of Athens university), the Grau brothers, Jones, Didring, and our first woman recruit, Sigrid Elgström of the Stockholm Institute. All passed through our hands in a space of twenty days. My feelings about it all were mixed. It was a relief to feel that the secret was spreading, and that Reich and I were no longer its sole custodians; but I was always afraid that someone might make a mistake and alert the parasites. Although I had convinced myself that they were not really dangerous, some instinct told me the importance of continued secrecy.

Some of the developments were extremely exciting. The Grau brothers, Louis and Heinrich, had always been close together, and already possessed a certain ability to communicate telepathically. They now outstripped us all in psychokinetic powers, and revealed that we might be underestimating the importance of PK. I was present in the antiquities room of the British Museum when they moved a marble block *weighing thirty tons* by concentrating in unison. The only others present were Iannis Lascaratos, Emlyn Jones, Georges Ribot, Kenneth Furneaux (the director of the archaeology section, whom I had 'initiated') and myself. The brothers explained that they did this by somehow reinforcing one another's efforts in a pulse rhythm. At the time, we were completely incapable of understanding them.

Before I go on to describe the first disaster that overtook us, I should say something more about PK, since it plays a part in my narrative. It was, of course, a simple and natural consequence of the new *purpose* given us to fight against the parasites. The first thing I realized when I started practising Husserlian disciplines was that human beings have been overlooking an extremely simple secret about existence, although it is obvious enough for anyone to see. The secret is this: that the poor quality of human life – and consciousness – is due to the feebleness of the beam of attention that we direct at the world. Imagine that you have a powerful searchlight, but it has no reflector inside it. When you turn it on, you get a light of sorts, but it rushes off in all directions, and a lot of it is absorbed by the inside of the searchlight. Now if you install a concave reflector, the beam is polarized, and stabs forward like a bullet or a spear. The beam immediately becomes ten times as powerful. But even this is only a half measure, for although every ray of light now follows the same path, the actual waves of light are ' out of step ', like an undisciplined army walking along a street. If you now pass the light through a ruby laser, the result is that the waves now ' march in step ', and their power is increased a thousand-fold – just as the rhythmic tramping of an army was able to bring down the walls of Jericho.

The human brain is a kind of searchlight that projects a beam of ' attention ' on the world. But it has always been like a searchlight without a reflector. Our attention shifts around from second to second; we do not really have the trick of focusing and concentrating the beam. And yet it *does* happen fairly often. For example, as Fleishman observed, the sexual orgasm is actually a focusing and concentrating of the ' beam ' of consciousness (or attention). The beam of attention suddenly carries more power, and the result is a feeling of intense pleasure. The ' inspiration ' of poets is exactly the same thing. By some fluke, some accidental adjustment of the mind, the beam of attention is polarized for a moment, and whatever it happens to be focused on appears to be transformed, touched with ' the glory and the freshness of a dream '. There is no need to add that so-called ' mystical ' visions are exactly the same thing, but with an accidental touch of the laser thrown in. When Jacob Boehme saw the sunlight reflected on a pewter bowl, and declared that he had seen all heaven, he was speaking the sober truth.

Human beings never realize that life is so dull because of the vagueness, the diffuseness, of their beam of attention – although, as I say, the secret has been lying at the end of their noses for centuries. And since 1800, the parasites have been doing their best to distract them from this discovery – a discovery that should have been *quite inevitable* after the age of Beethoven and Goethe and Wordsworth. They achieved this mainly by encouraging the human habit of vagueness and the tendency to waste time on trivialities. A man has a sudden glimpse of a great idea; for a moment, his mind *focuses*. At this point, habit steps in. His stomach complains of being empty, or his throat complains of dryness, and a false little voice whispers: 'Go and satisfy your physical needs, and then you'll be able to concentrate twice as well'. He obeys — and immediately forgets the great idea.

The moment man stumbles on the fact that his attention is a 'beam', (or, as Husserl put it, that consciousness is 'intentional') he has learned the fundamental secret. Now all he has to learn is how to polarize that beam. It is the 'polarized' beam that exerts PK effects.

Now, what the Grau brothers had discovered, quite accidentally, was how to use each other's minds as ruby lasers, to 'phase' the beam. They were by no means expert at it; they wasted about 99% of the beam's power. But even the remaining 1% was enough to move thirty tons with the greatest of ease. It would have been enough to move a block weighing five hundred tons if we had had one available.

And now to the night of October the 14th, when catastrophe struck us. I have no way of knowing who was responsible for alerting the parasites. It was probably Georges Ribot, a rather strange little man who had been initiated by Gioberti. Ribot had written various books on telepathy, magic, spiritualism, and so on, with titles like *The Hidden Temple* and *From Atlantis to Hiroshima*, and founded the magazine *Les Horizons de L'Avenir*. It would perhaps be unfair to say that Gioberti showed a lack of judgement in choosing him. Ribot was a man of keen intellect and a good mathematician. His books revealed that he had come very close to suspecting the existence of the mind parasites. On the other hand, they were too speculative, not sufficiently scientific. He would pass from Atlantis to atomic physics, from primitive tribal ceremonies to cybernetics. He would spoil a sound argument on evolution by dragging in some unverified 'fact' from spiritualist literature. He would cite cranks and scientists in the same footnote. He came to Diyarbakir especially to see me – a small man with a thin nervous face and intensely penetrating black eyes. He gave me an immediate sense of being less reliable than the others I had met, in spite of his intelligence and knowledge. His movements were too nervous and fast. I had a feeling that he was less stable than the others, less mentally secure. Reich expressed this by saying: 'He's not indifferent enough.'

At ten o'clock at night, I was making notes in my room. I suddenly had that 'shivery' feeling that told me that the parasites were present. It was exactly as in my Percy Street rooms. I surmised that they were making some kind of periodic check on me, so I simply merged my new personality into my old one, and began to think about a chess problem. I deliberately thought in slow-motion, examining each aspect of the problem minutely, although my mind could have leapt to a conclusion instantly. Halfway through, I allowed my thoughts to be distracted, and got up to get myself a fruit juice. (I had ceased to drink alcohol; the stimulus could now be achieved quite easily by a momentary act of concentration.) Then I pretended that I had lost my grip on the problem, and started laboriously from the beginning. After half an hour or so of this, I yawned and allowed my mind to grow tired. All this time, I remained aware that they were watching me, and at a deeper level of consciousness than in Percy Street. A year ago, I would not even have experienced depression under such observation; it was completely outside the range of conscious or unconscious awareness.

After I had been in bed for ten minutes, I realized they had gone, and began to speculate on what they could have done to me if they had decided to 'attack'. It was difficult to tell, but I felt that my mind was strong enough to repulse an exceptionally strong attack.

At midnight, my screen rang. It was Reich, and he looked worried.

106

'Have they been to you?'

'Yes. They went an hour ago.'

Reich said: 'They only just left me. It's my first real experience of them, and I don't like it. They're stronger than we thought.'

'I don't know. I think it's some kind of routine check up. Did you manage to hide your thoughts?'

'Oh, yes. Luckily I was working on these Abhoth inscriptions, so I simply had to concentrate on them and think at half speed.'

I said: 'Ring me if you need any help. I think we might try putting our minds in phase, like the Grau brothers. It might work.'

I went back to sleep. I even took the precaution of allowing my consciousness to drift into sleep, in the old way, instead of shutting it off like a light.

I woke up from sleep with a feeling of oppression like a hangover, or the beginnings of some illness. My mind felt rusty and cramped, as my body might have felt cramped if I had fallen asleep in a cold and damp spot. Instantly, I knew that the time for bluff was over. They had moved in quietly while I was asleep, and had me prisoner. I was like a man held tightly by both arms and legs.

Now it had happened, it was not as unpleasant as I had expected. Their actual presence was not disgusting, as I had always believed. It was alien, and had an element that I might describe as 'metallic'.

I had no idea of resisting. For the moment, I was like a man under arrest whose best chance of survival depends on pleading to his captors that they are mistaken. So I reacted just as I would have reacted a year ago: with a certain fear, with bewilderment, but with a fundamental lack of panic, a certainty that it was some oppression that I would throw off with a dose of aspirin. I let my mind search my actions during the previous day to try to account for this feeling of illness.

107

For about half an hour, nothing else happened. I simply lay there, quite passive and not too worried, wondering if they would relax. I felt that I could exert my strength if necessary, and throw them off.

Then I began to realize that this was no use. They *knew* that I knew; they knew I was playing possum. And, as if they sensed my realization, a new stage began. They began to put pressure on my mind, the kind of pressure that would simply have driven me insane in the old days. Just as physical nausea produces a sense of physical oppression, so their pressure produced a sense of mental oppression, a kind of nausea.

I obviously had to resist, but I decided not to show my hand yet. I resisted passively, as if I were not even aware of their pressure. They probably had a sensation of trying to move a hundred ton block by pushing it. The pressure increased, and I felt quietly confident. I knew I had the strength to resist fifty times this much.

But half an hour later, I felt as though my mind was supporting a load the size of Mount Everest. I still had plenty of reserve strength, but if this carried on, I might exhaust it. There was nothing but to show my hand. So with an effort like a man bursting his bonds, I threw them off. I focused the beam of my attention to about the intensity of a sexual orgasm, and blasted it at them. I could have increased it to ten times that amount, but I still wanted to keep them guessing about my strength. I was still calm and un-panicked. In a sense, I was almost enjoying this contest. If I won, it meant that in future I did not have to limit my strength carefully, because they now knew in any case.

The result of my first effort was disappointing. The weight vanished and they scattered; but I had a feeling that they were unhurt. It was like trying to hit shadows. It would have been infinitely satisfying to feel that I'd hit them, like a boxer landing a punch; but obviously, I hadn't.

Their attack commenced again immediately. This time, it

108

was so sudden and violent that I was forced to parry it from an unprepared position. One might say that I was like a householder facing an attack from a horde of tramps. I had a feeling that these things belonged to some 'lower' order, that they were a kind of vermin that had no right in my mind. Like rats from sewers, they had decided that they had the strength to attack, and it was my business to show them that they would not be tolerated. I was not afraid; I felt that they were on my 'territory'. As they came back, I lashed out at them, and felt them scatter again.

I have occasionally been asked by the uninitiated whether I actually 'saw' them, or felt that they had a definite shape. The answer is no. My sensations can best be envisaged if you imagine how it feels when you are hot and tired, and everything seems to be going wrong. Every time you start to cross the road, a bus almost runs over your feet. You feel as if the whole universe were hostile, like two lines of thugs between whom you have to run a gauntlet. Your feeling of security vanishes, and it seems that everything about your life is horribly brittle and destructible. Well, this gives an idea of the form that the attacks took. In the old days, I would have assumed they were merely attacks of pessimism and self-pity, and would have promptly found something to worry about, so that they seemed reasonable. We all fight such battles a hundred times a day, and those who win them conclusively do so by hurling aside their tendency to be negative, to worry about life, and by thinking in terms of conquest, of important purposes. We all know this trick of drawing on the 'secret life' inside us. My training over the past months had simply made this secret life far more accessible. My strength came from optimism, from 'positive thinking', if I might borrow that dubious phrase.

For perhaps an hour, I skirmished with them. I did not let myself worry about what would happen if there were millions of them, enough to keep attacking me for weeks until my mind was exhausted. When this thought presented itself, I suppressed it. And yet, of course, it was the basic danger.

By five o'clock, I was a little tired, but not at all depressed. It was then that I got the impression that they had received reinforcements, that they were massing for attack. This time, I decided to risk letting them get in close. I wanted to find if I could hurt them. So I let them press in on me, like a great crowd. I let them press closer and closer, until I felt I was suffocating. It was a terrifying sensation, like allowing someone to close a vice on your hand. The weight increased. Still I made no resistance. Then, when it seemed to become too heavy to bear, I gathered all the force of my mind, and lashed out at them, as if firing a cannon right into the midst of them. This time, there was no mistake. They may have been as light as a swarm of flies, but they were massed so thickly that they could not retreat quickly enough, and I had the satisfying feeling of damaging a large number.

Now, for half an hour, there was peace. They were still there, but it was obvious that they were badly shaken. I discovered later why this was. With my months of preparation, I had learned to call on an inner-strength that would be the mental equivalent of a hydrogen bomb. It was the first time I had ever used it, so even I had no idea of its power. They had mobbed me like a horde of rats mobbing a kitten – and then discovered they were attacking a full grown tiger. No wonder they were startled.

I also felt well satisfied. Although I had exerted my full strength in repelling them, I had not exhausted myself. I felt as fresh and strong as ever, and the exhilaration of their defeat made me feel as if I could carry on for weeks.

But as the daylight began to come through the curtains, I knew I was facing something for which I had not been prepared. It was a curious sensation, like suddenly feeling cold water round your feet, then feeling it slowly rising up your legs. It took me some time to realize that they were attacking from some part of my mind *of whose existence I was*

110

unaware. I had been strong because I was fighting them out of knowledge, but I should have known that my knowledge of mind was pitifully small. I was like an astronomer who knows the solar system, and thinks he knows the universe.

What the parasites were doing was to attack me *from below my knowledge of myself.* It is true that I had given some small thought to the matter; but I had – rightly – postponed it as a study for a more advanced period. I had reflected often enough that our human life is based completely on ' premises ' that we take for granted. A child takes its parents and its home for granted; later, it comes to take its country and its society for granted. We need these supports to begin with. A child without parents and a regular home grows up feeling insecure. A child that has had a good home may later learn to criticize its parents, or even reject them altogether (although this is unlikely); but it only does so when it is strong enough to stand alone.

All original thinkers develop by kicking away these ' supports ' one by one. They may continue to love their parents and their country, but they love from a position of strength – a strength that began in rejection.

In fact, though, human beings never really learn to stand alone. They are lazy, and prefer supports. A man may be a fearlessly original mathematician, and yet be slavishly dependent on his wife. He may be a powerful free thinker, yet derive a great deal more comfort than he would admit from the admiration of a few friends and disciples. In short, human beings never question *all* their supports; they question a few, and continue to take the rest for granted.

Now I had been so absorbed in the adventure of entering new mental continents, rejecting my old personality and its assumptions, that I had been quite unaware that I was still leaning heavily on dozens of ordinary assumptions. For example, although I felt my identity had changed, I still had a strong feeling of identity. And our most fundamental sense of identity comes from an anchor that lies at the bottom of a very deep sea. I still looked upon myself as a member of the human race. I still looked upon myself as an inhabitant of the solar system and the universe in space and time. I took space and time for granted. I did not ask where I had been before my birth or after my death. I did not even recognize the problem of my own death; it was something I left 'to be explored later'.

What the parasites now did was to go to these deep moorings of my identity, and proceed to shake them. I cannot express it more clearly than this. They did not actually, so to speak, pull up the anchors. That was beyond their powers. But they shook the chains, so that I suddenly became aware of an insecurity on a level I had taken completely for granted. I found myself asking: Who am I? In the deepest sense. Just as a bold thinker dismisses patriotism and religion, so I dismissed all the usual things that gave me an 'identity': the accident of my time and place of birth, the accident of my being a human being rather than a dog or a fish, the accident of my powerful instinct to cling to life. Having thrown off all these accidental 'trappings', I stood naked as pure consciousness confronting the universe. But here I became aware that this so-called 'pure consciousness' was as arbitrary as my name. It could not confront the universe without sticking labels on it. How could it be 'pure consciousness' when I saw that object as a book, that one as a table? It was still my tiny human identity looking out of my eyes. And if I tried to get beyond it, everything went blank.

I was not doing all this thinking for fun. I was trying to fight my way down to some solid bedrock on which I could take my stand against them. They had simply been cunning enough to show me that I was standing over an abyss. For my mind leapt on to recognize that we also take space and time for granted, although death takes us beyond them. I saw that what I call 'existence' means existence in space and time, and that this universe of space and time is not an absolute. Suddenly, *everything became absurd*. For the first

112

time, a dreadful sense of insecurity and weakness gripped my stomach. I saw that everything I take for granted in this universe can be questioned – that they could all be a trick. As a thinker, I had got into the old romantic habit of feeling that the mind is beyond the accidents of the body, that it is somehow eternal and free; that the body may be trivial and particular, but the mind is universal and general. This attitude makes the mind an eternal spectator, beyond fear. But now I suddenly felt: ' But if the universe itself is arbitrary, then my mind is as casual and destructible as my body '. This is the point where one remembers the times of sickness and delirium, when the mind seems altogether less durable than the body, when one suspects that it is mainly the body's toughness that is preventing the mind from disintegrating.

Suddenly, abysses of emptiness were open beneath my feet. It did not even produce fear; that would be too human a reaction. It was like contact with an icy reality that makes everything human seem a masquerade, *that makes life itself seem a masquerade*. It seemed to strike at the heart of my life, something I had thought untouchable. I felt like a king who has always given orders and had them obeyed, and who suddenly falls into the hands of barbarians who drive a sword into his bowels. It was so horribly and instantly real that it negated everything I had ever been, made everything an illusion. In that moment, it became totally unimportant whether the parasites won or not. All my strength, all my courage, ran away. I felt like a ship that has struck a rock, and suddenly realized that it is vulnerable.

The parasites did not attack. They watched me, as they might have watched a poisoned animal wriggling. I tried to gather my forces to prepare for attack, but I felt paralysed, exhausted. It seemed pointless. My mind's strength was against me. Instead of flickering inattentively, as in the old days, it contemplated this emptiness unblinkingly.

They made a mistake not to attack then. They would have overcome me, for I had lost most of my strength, and had not time to recover it. This was how they had killed Karel Weissman – I knew this with certainty. For this vision of futility, of nothingness, also brings the thought that death cannot be worse than this. One feels that life means clinging to the body and its illusions. One looks back on the body just as one looks down on the earth from a space ship; but in this case, there is a feeling that there would be no point in returning.

Yes, they should have attacked then. Perhaps Karel's death convinced them that I would die in the same way, by committing suicide. But there was no such temptation in my case, for my mind was free of the neurotic pressures that would have made me dream about release. Only a neurotic woman faints when someone attacks her; a strong-minded woman knows that this is no solution.

Now a thought came that helped to turn the tide. It was this: that since these creatures had deliberately induced this feeling of total meaninglessness, they must be in some way *beyond* it. As soon as this idea floated into my mind, strength began to return. I saw that they had set out to get me into this state, just as turtle hunters used to turn them on their backs; they knew that this was a direction from which human beings were vulnerable. But if this was so, then presumably they themselves knew it was some kind of illusion, this sense of emptiness. My mind was doing its best, but it was making a mistake. An adult can easily browbeat a small child by taking advantage of his ignorance. He could, for example, drive a child insane by filling his mind with horror stories – of the Dracula-Frankenstein variety – and then pointing to Buchenwald and Belsen to prove that the world is even more horrible than these. In a sense it would be true, but it would take an adult to see through the fallacy: that Belsen and Buchenwald are not *necessary* horrors in the nature of the universe; that they can be fought by human decency. Perhaps these creatures were taking advantage of my ignorance in the same way? My reasoning *seemed* accurate enough:

that our ability to go on living depends upon a series of supports that have the nature of illusions. But, then, a child can cease to believe that its parents are infallible without ceasing to love them. In other words, there is still a reality left there to love, when the illusions have vanished. Could it be that this awful agony – or, rather, this awful lack of agony, this feeling of utter coldness and reality – was no more dangerous than a child's pain when it falls down?

I grasped at this possibility and clung to it. Then another thought came that strengthened me. I realized that when I contemplated this alien 'universe', and felt it to be arbitrary and absurd, I was making the oldest of human errors: of believing that the word 'universe' means 'universe *out there*'. The mind, as I well knew, was a universe of its own.

They had made their first mistake in not attacking me when I was shattered and exhausted. They now made an even greater one. They saw that I was somehow recovering, and they attacked in force.

I was panic-stricken. I knew I had not the strength to fight them off. This glance into the abyss had drained off all my courage; now it had to seep back slowly.

At that moment, the full implications of my argument about the child dawned on me. A child can be browbeaten in its ignorance because it underestimates its strength. It does not realize that it is *potentially* an adult, perhaps a scientist, a poet, a leader.

In a flash, I saw that perhaps I was doing the same thing. And I suddenly remembered Karel's words about his first battle with the parasites: about how his own deepest life forces had rallied to beat them. Were there actually deeper levels of strength that I had not yet called upon? At the same moment, I remembered my frequent feeling, over the past months, that there was some strange force of luck on our side – what I used to call 'the god of archaeology', some *benevolent* force whose purpose was to preserve life.

No doubt a religious man would have identified that force

with God. For me, this was irrelevant. I only knew suddenly that I might have an unexpected ally in this fight. And as I had this thought, it was as if I heard the trumpets of an army coming to relieve me. The most frenzied exaltation I have ever known swept through me. No form of emotional expression could have been adequate for that sense of relief and triumph; crying or laughing or screaming would have been absurd, like trying to empty the sea with a thimble. As soon as it started, it spread like an atomic explosion. I was almost more afraid of it than of the parasites. Yet I also knew that *this power was being released by myself*. It was not really some ' third force ', outside me and the parasites. It was some great *passive* benevolence that I had contacted, something that had no power of action in itself, but which had to be approached and used.

I overcame my fear and seized it. I clamped my teeth together and grasped this power with my will. To my amazement, I could control it. I turned my attention-beam on the enemy, and then let the power blast down it, dazzled and drunk by it, seeing meanings that were beyond anything I had ever suspected, and quite unable to grasp them in any way. All my words, ideas, concepts, were like leaves in a hurricane. The parasites saw it coming too late. Obviously, in a sense they were as inexperienced as I was. It was the blind fighting the blind. The inexpressibly searing blast hit them like some enormous flame thrower, destroying them as though they were earwigs. I had no desire to use it for more than a few seconds. Somehow, it would have seemed unfair, like using a machine gun on children. I deliberately turned it off, and felt wave after wave of it roar through me, crackling around my head like sparks of electricity. I could actually see a sort of blue-green glow emanating from my chest. It went on and on in waves, like thunder, but I no longer used it. I knew there was no reason to use it further. I closed my eyes, and let my body take it, aware that it could destroy me. Gradually it subsided, and in spite of my ecstasy and gratitude, I was glad to see it go. It had been far too great.

Then I was back in the room – for I had been elsewhere for many hours. The sound of traffic came from below. The electric clock said half past nine. The bed was soaked with sweat – so wet that it seemed as if I had emptied a bath of water over it. My eyesight was affected; I tended to see slightly double, as if everything had an outer ring of light. Things seemed incredibly bright and clear, and I understood for the first time the visual effects produced by mescalin on Aldous Huxley.

I also knew that I was in another kind of danger: that I must not try and think about what had happened, because I would only get hopelessly confused and depressed. In fact, the danger was greater than it had been half an hour or so before, when I had looked into an abyss. So I determinedly directed my thoughts elsewhere, to everyday things. I did not want to ask myself why I was fighting the mind parasites if I had such strength, why human beings are fighting life when they could overcome every problem instantaneously. I did not want to speculate whether the whole thing was some kind of play. I hurried to the bathroom and washed my face. I was startled that I looked so fresh and normal in the mirror. There was no physical sign of the conflict, except that I seemed slightly thinner. When I stood on the bathroom scale, I had another surprise: I was two stones lighter.

The telescreen rang. It was the head of A.I.U. I looked at him as if he was from another world. I also noted that he looked somehow relieved to see me. He told me that reporters had been trying to contact me since eight o'clock. For twenty of my colleagues had died in the night: Gioberti, Curtis, Remizov, Shlaf, Herzog, Klebnikov, Ames, Thomson, Didring, Lascaratos, Spencefield, Sigrid Elgström – everybody, in fact, except the Grau brothers, Fleishman, Reich, myself – and Georges Ribot. The first four had apparently died of heart failure. Sigrid Elgström had slashed her wrists, then her throat. Klebnikov and Lascaratos had jumped from high windows. Thomson had apparently broken his neck in some kind of epileptic fit. Herzog had shot his whole family and then himself. Others had taken poison or overdoses of drugs. Two died of brain lesions.

Reubke was in a state of nerves, thinking about the bad publicity for A.I.U., since almost every one of the victims had been my guests – and guests of A.I.U. – in the past weeks; Reubke had met most of them himself. I soothed him as best I could – I was shaken myself – and told him not to allow any reporters to get on to me. When he said he had tried to ring Reich, but got no reply, I felt as though my stomach had turned to ice. Reaction was setting in heavily now. I would have preferred to sleep. But I used my own special dialling code, and rang Reich's number. When his face appeared on the screen, my relief was unspeakable. Reich's first words were:

' Thank God you're all right.'

' I'm all right, but how about you? You look awful?'

' Did they come to you in the night again?'

' Yes, all night. They came to all of us.'

In five minutes, I was with him – pausing only long enough to tell Reubke that Reich was all right. But when I saw him, I realized this was an overstatement. He looked like a man who is just recovering from a six months' illness. His flesh had become the colour of cooked veal. He looked older.

Reich's experience had been very much the same as mine – with one significant variation. They had not tried the ' total undermining ' technique with him. They had merely pressed him hard all night, hurling wave after wave at him. Towards morning, they had produced a kind of crack in his mental armour, a leak in his energy tanks. It was after this that he became so exhausted. And then, when he had begun to believe that defeat was inevitable, the attacks had stopped.

I had no difficulty in guessing when this had happened: at

118

the time when I released my 'energy blast' at them. Reich verified this. It had happened about half an hour before I rang him. Before that, he had heard the screen ringing, but had been too exhausted to do anything about it.

My news about the others depressed him, but then my own story brought back his hope and courage. I tried my best to explain how they had succeeded in undermining me, and how I had called upon the god-force to defeat them. It was all he needed – the knowledge that he was mistaken to think we were helpless against them. The characteristic of 'initiates' of the phenomenological method is that they can recover from physical or mental catastrophes at a great speed – naturally, since they are in direct contact with the sources of power that drive all human beings. In half an hour, Reich no longer looked ill, and he was talking as excitedly as I was myself.

It took me most of the morning to explain to him exactly how they had undermined me, and how it could be combated. For what it involved was teaching Reich to 'undermine' himself voluntarily, to examine his own foundations of identity. I discovered that his temperament was very different from mine fundamentally. In certain respects he was far stronger, in others, weaker.

At midday, we were interrupted by Reubke, who came up to see us. By this time, every newspaper in the world was headlining the 'night of suicide', and speculating about the part Reich and I had played. I was told that the whole A.I.U. factory – covering eight hundred acres – had become unapproachable because of thousands of helicopters waiting outside – journalists.

A quick mental probe told me that Reubke was not strong enough to be told the full truth. I was tempted to take over his mind completely – I had realized that I could do this since early this morning. A feeling of 'respect for the individual' withheld me. Instead, we told him a story that was close to the truth, but easier for him to grasp.

What it amounted to was telling him that the Anti-Kadath Society had been right: our digging at Karatepe had disturbed immense and dangerous forces: the Great Old Ones themselves. The rest of the story was more or less true: that these creatures had a psychic power that could drive men insane. We told him that their aim was to destroy the human race, or at least to enslave them so that the Elder Race could again rule the solar system. But so far, they were not strong enough. If we could defeat them in time, they could be finally expelled from our galaxy, or perhaps even destroyed completely.

What we had done was to turn the truth about the parasites into a child's fable – something that could be easily grasped, something not too frightening. We even gave these creatures a name – the Tsathogguans – borrowed from Lovecraft's mythology.

We ended by placing the question solemnly before him: should the human race be told of its danger, or would this create a panic that would be a far greater danger? Reubke turned the colour of putty, and walked up and down the room gasping – he was trying to hold off an asthmatic attack, and I was helping him – and finally said that he thought we had to present our story to the world. It was interesting to see that there was no question of disbelief: our two minds had complete power over him.

But the 'Tsathogguans' were still one jump ahead of us, as we found out an hour later. Georges Ribot made a statement to United Press in which he accused Reich and myself of being murderers and confidence tricksters. Part of his statement ran as follows:

'One month ago, I was approached by Vincent Gioberti, the assistant of Professor Sigmund Fleishman at the University of Berlin; he told me that a small group of scientists had formed a World Safety League, and had suggested me as a member. In due course, I was introduced to other members (here the others are listed), and to the co-founders of the League, Wolfgang Reich and Gilbert Austin, the men who discovered Kadath. Their discovery had given them an idea for saving the world: they had decided that the whole world must be united against some common enemy. This common enemy would be the " Great Old Ones " of Kadath . . . All of us had to agree to support this deception whatever happened. Reich and Austin believed that only a body of well-known scientists could convince the world of their fantastic story . . . I was asked to undergo hypnosis, like the others, but I refused. Finally, under the threat of death, I agreed to a single session. My own hypnotic powers enabled me to deceive them that I had become their slave . . .'

In short, Ribot claimed that what had happened in the night was the result of a unilateral suicide pact, inspired by myself and Reich. The aim of the pact: to convince the world beyond all shadow of doubt that it was facing a dangerous enemy. Reich and I had claimed that we would die with the others, and that our revelations about the Great Old Ones would be published after our deaths.

It was fantastic, but ingenious. It all sounded impossible: but then, the suicide of twenty leading scientists was also impossible, and our own alternative explanation was equally fantastic and impossible.

If it had not been for my own personal victory over the parasites, this would have been the most depressing moment of all. Twenty-four hours ago, everything had seemed perfect; we had reckoned that it would take another month before we were ready to make our announcement to the world, and by then we would have been a formidable team. Now almost everything was ruined, and Ribot had become an ally – or a victim – of the parasites, turning our own best-thought-out plans against us. As far as convincing the world was concerned, the parasites were definitely in the lead. We had no proof of their existence, and they would take care that no proof was forthcoming. If we announced our story about the Tsathogguans now, Ribot would simply challenge us to produce any proof that they were not our own invention. The only people who would believe us would be the Anti-Kadath Society!

It was Reich who said suddenly: ' It's no use sitting here brooding about it. We take things too slowly, and these creatures get ahead of us. Speed is essential.'

' What do you suggest?'

' We've got to get the Fleishman and the Grau brothers together, and find out how badly they're hurt. If they're as exhausted as I was four hours ago, the parasites could destroy them now.'

We tried to contact Berlin on the telescreen; it was impossible. The number of calls coming and going around Diyarbakir ruined long distance reception. We called Reubke, and told him that we needed a rocket plane immediately to go to Berlin, and that total secrecy had to be observed. It was obvious that Reubke was worried about Ribot's ' confession ', so we wasted ten minutes in re-energizing his mind. It was disappointing work; he was so mentally flabby that it was like trying to fill a bucket with a hole in the bottom. Still, we managed it by appealing to his greed and lust for celebrity, pointing out that, as our chief ally, his name would go down in history, and that his firm could hardly fail to prosper. Together with Reubke, we arranged a small deception to keep reporters on the wrong track. Reich and I made a tele-recording, in which Reich answered the telescreen, and I was visible behind him; then Reich shouted irritably at the operator that no calls from outside were to be put through. We arranged that this recording should be shown about half an hour after we had left – some reporter would be put through ' by accident '.

The ruse worked. We were actually able to watch ourselves on the rocket's television as we arrived in Berlin. The reporter who got this ' scoop ' had tele-recorded it at his end, and within twenty minutes it was being broadcast from the

Diyarbakir television station. There had apparently been much speculation about whether we were alive, in spite of Reubke's statement to the press, so this item of news was immediately given widespread publicity. As a consequence, one or two people who thought they recognized us at the Berlin Airport must have decided they were mistaken.

At Fleishman's house, we had no alternative except to reveal our identity. The place was surrounded by reporters, and we would never have got in. But here we both discovered a rather useful aspect of our psychokinetic powers. In a way, we were able to make ourselves ' invisible ': that is, we were able to intercept any attention directed towards us, and turn it aside, so that people simply did not notice us. We actually managed to get as far as ringing Fleishman's front door bell before we were recognized. Then the rush started. Luckily, Fleishman's voice spoke to us out of the intercom, and the moment we identified ourselves, the door opened. A moment later, we were inside, and the reporters were rattling the door and shouting messages through the letter box.

Fleishman looked better than we expected, but he was obviously exhausted. In a few minutes, we learned that his story was identical with Reich's – a long night of skirmishes, and sudden relief at exactly eight-twenty-five that morning – allowing for the two hour time lag between Berlin and Diyarbakir. This raised my spirits considerably: at least I had saved the lives of two of my colleagues, and saved the night from complete disaster.

Fleishman was also able to tell us about the Grau brothers, who were at present in Potsdam, their home. He had been able to contact them that morning, before reporters began jamming all out-going calls . . . They owed their safety to the accident of being telepathically linked. Just as they were able to use one another's minds as amplifiers for their PK powers, so they were able to draw upon one another's strength in their night battle. Fleishman gathered that the parasites had also attempted to ' undermine ' them as they had undermined me, but, again, their telepathic link was their strength. I learned later that they had not 'faced' the problem of non-identity, as I had. They had simply encouraged one another in refusing to consider it, in looking away from it. The undermining technique depends very much upon the victim being alone.

The next problem seemed almost insoluble: how to get to Potsdam and collect the Grau brothers – or, at least, how to get them to come to Diyarbakir immediately. The house was surrounded by reporters, and a dozen helicopters simply hovered overhead. When the news of our presence spread, these increased to about a hundred. Any attempt to contact Potsdam would send reporters scurrying there, since local calls were easier to tap than long distance ones. As far as we knew, the name of the Grau brothers had not yet been dragged into the story, so they probably still had some freedom of movement.

It was Fleishman who saw the solution. After an hour with us, he was already feeling better; the process of re-energizing his mind was far simpler than in the case of Reubke. The story of my victory had upon him the same effect as upon Reich – of restoring all the old optimism and purpose. And now Fleishman suddenly remarked:

'We've learned one interesting thing about the parasites. It's wrong to think of them as existing in some kind of space. The crowd attacking me here must have been more or less the same crowd who were attacking you two in Diyarbakir – otherwise the attacks wouldn't all have stopped at the same moment.'

This had also struck myself and Reich earlier. But Fleishman saw another consequence.

'In that case, we're mistaken to think about the mind in terms of physical space. In the mental sense, all the space in the universe is somehow compressed to a point. They don't have to travel to get from here to Diyarbakir. They're already in both places at once.'

124

'And in Potsdam too,' Reich said.

All of us saw the consequences at once. If the parasites were, in a sense, in Potsdam at the moment, *then so were we.*

Of course, it should have been obvious! Human beings exist in the physical world only in so far as they have no power to enter their own minds. A man who can withdraw into himself on a long train journey has escaped time and space, while the man who stares out of the window and yawns with boredom has to live through every minute and every mile. Our power to fight the mind parasites lay in precisely that ability to descend into ourselves and fight them on their own ground. A man who swims on the surface is an easy prey for sharks, but a diver who swims under the surface with a mask and a spear is on terms of equality with the shark. Well in so far as we could descend into our own minds, we were able to enter that same realm of spacelessness and timelessness as the parasites. The brothers could communicate with one another telepathically; why shouldn't we be able to communicate with them?

There was a simple answer: we had no idea of how to go about it. We knew that it must involve the same kind of faculty as psychokinesis, but that told us nothing at all.

So we turned off the lights and experimented, sitting around a table. To anyone entering the room, it would have looked as if we were holding a seance, sitting with bowed heads, our hands touching.

I tried first. As soon as we had sat down, I sent a mental signal: 'Are you ready?' to them. There was no result. Then suddenly, with a shock of pleasure, I seemed to hear Reich's voice inside my chest saying: 'Are you ready?' I sent back: 'Yes, can you hear me?' His voice came back: 'Not very clearly.'

It took Fleishman some ten minutes before he could enter into our game. By that time, Reich and I were communicating fairly clearly. This was obviously because, like the Grau brothers, we had grown adjusted to one another. However, after some time, we were able to pick up Fleishman's thought waves, sounding like a voice shouting in the distance.

We now knew we could communicate with one another: but could we communicate with the Graus?

A long and exhausting hour now went past, and I felt like someone lost on a mountain, shouting for help. I kept sending out mental signals for Louis and Heinrich Grau, but these signals kept turning into mere words, as if I was shouting their names aloud. What was needed was to project the naked *urge* to contact them, without words.

Suddenly, Reich said, 'I think I'm getting something.' We all concentrated hard, trying to send back a 'Message received' signal. And then, with an astounding clarity that made us all jump, a voice seemed to shout in our ears: 'I am getting you. What do you want?' We looked at one another in astonishment and triumph, then closed our eyes again and redoubled our concentration. The loud, clear voice said: 'Not all at once. One at a time. Reich, will you signal? You seem to be clearest.'

It was as if the clear one-way communication from Potsdam to Berlin cleared the line the other way. We could feel Reich's mind pumping out messages like spurts of energy. 'Can you get to Diyarbakir?' He had to repeat the message a dozen times. Then, listening to him we found ourselves making a certain effort in sympathy. To begin with, the Graus protested 'One at a time.' Then, suddenly, it was as if we fell into step with Reich, using our own mental amplifiers simply to amplify *his* signal and send it on. Immediately, the voice of the Graus said: 'That's better. I'm getting you clearly now.' From then on there was no difficulty. We were even able to give them a resumé of our situation, just as if we were speaking on the telephone. During all this time, *we were not in the room*. We were totally self-absorbed, like men in prayer. And I suddenly realized that the reason for the bad amplification was that I was not deep enough in my own mind; I was too near the surface. The trouble was a simple one: if I sank too deep into my mind, I tended to fall asleep. Language and meaning belong to the realm of the body. It is as difficult to carry them into the depths of one's mind as to carry logical thought into a dream. I mention this because it was at this moment that I first became clearly aware of the immensity of our ignorance. Those deep areas of the mind are inhabited mainly by memories and dreams, which drift by like great fishes. It is tremendously difficult to preserve any sense of purpose at that depth, to distinguish reality from illusion. And yet for really efficient telepathy, one has to 'send' from this depth.

However, on this occasion, it did not matter. Reich, Fleishman and I reinforced one another. It is only in an experience like this that one can recognize the full meaning of the phrase 'we are members of one another'.

When we had finished talking with the Graus, we all felt strangely happy and refreshed, as if waking from a deep and peaceful sleep. Fleishman looked his old self again. His wife, who brought us in some coffee, and was obviously trying to control her hostility to Reich and myself, looked at him with amazement, and obviously revised her ideas about us. It was interesting, incidentally, to note that Fleishman's obvious tenderness for her – she was thirty years his junior, and had only married him a year ago – communicated itself to Reich and myself, so that we looked at her with a proprietary fondness that combined lust and an intimate knowledge of her body. She had simply dropped into our telepathic circle, and become, in a sense, the wife of all three of us. (I should also note that the lust experienced by Reich and myself was not the usual male desire to possess a strange female, for we had already, so to speak, possessed her, through Fleishman.)

By three in the morning, the reporters in helicopters had grown tired of waiting for us. Besides, their numbers were more than the City's Air Safety Regulations allowed. But the crowd outside the front door was undiminished, and the street was lined with automobiles containing sleeping reporters. We went up to the attic, and placed a ladder against the skylight window. At three-twenty, there was the sound of a helicopter above the house, and we quickly opened the window. With some manoeuvring, the rope ladder was dropped into the room; then Fleishman, myself and Reich clambered up it as fast as we could, before the reporters below found out what was happening. The Grau brothers pulled us to safety, and pulled up the ladder, then the helicopter set off at top speed for the airfield. The operation was perfect. The reporters in the street were certain that we could have no way of summoning a helicopter, since they carried interception devices in their cars (strictly illegal, of course). So if any of them noticed the helicopter, they probably assumed it was another reporter, or perhaps a patrol of the Air Safety Council. At all events, we reached the airport with no sign of pursuit. The pilot had radioed ahead to the pilot of the rocket. By three-thirty-five, we were on our way to Paris. We had decided that our next business lay with Georges Ribot.

It was just after dawn when we landed at Le Bourget. We could have landed at the more convenient floating airport above the Champs-Elysées, but it would have involved radioing for permission, and this might have alerted reporters. Instead, we took a helicab into the centre of Paris from Le Bourget, and were there in twenty minutes.

Now there were five of us, we were almost impregnable as far as casual recognition went. With our minds ' in series ', we were able to form a kind of wall to divert the attention of anyone who happened to look at us. People could ' see ' us, of course, but they could not look *at* us. The faculty of understanding or grasping follows that of perception (as you can see if you read something with your mind elsewhere). Most objects we look at are not properly registered, because they are not worth noticing. We merely had to prevent the

' attention ' of any onlooker from ' closing ' on us – the same principle as jamming a stick in a dog's mouth to prevent him from biting. We were virtually invisible as we walked through Paris.

Our one hope lay in surprise. If the parasites were observing us, then they would make sure that we never got to Georges Ribot, for he could be warned hours before we arrived. On the other hand, they had sustained a considerable defeat the night before, and might well be off their guard. This is what we hoped.

We only had to pick up a newspaper to discover where he was, for Ribot was now a celebrity on a scale he had never known before. An abandoned copy of *Paris-Soir* told us that Ribot was in the Curel Clinic on the Boulevard Haussman, suffering from some kind of nervous collapse. We knew how to interpret this.

It was now necessary to use force, although we were still strongly opposed to the idea. The clinic was too small for us to get in unnoticed. But the hour – five in the morning – ensured that there would be few people around. A sleepy porter looked resentfully out of his office, and five minds clamped on him, seizing him far more powerfully than our five pairs of hands could have done. He gaped at us, incapable of understanding what had happened. Fleishman asked him softly: ' Do you know which room Ribot is in?' He nodded in a dazed manner – we had to relax our grip even to allow him to do that. ' Take us to him,' Fleishman said. The man pressed the automatic door opener, and led us in. A ward sister hurried forward saying: ' Where do you think you're going?' A moment later, she was also smartly preceding us along the corridors. We asked her why there were no reporters.

She replied: ' M. Ribot is giving a press conference at nine.' She had the presence of mind to add: ' I think you might have waited until then.'

We met two night nurses, but they must have assumed

our visit was in order. Ribot's room was at the very top of the building – a special private room. The doors to this section opened only by a special code. Luckily, the night porter knew it.

Fleishman said quietly: 'Now, madame, we shall have to ask you to wait in this outer room, and not to try to escape. We shall do the patient no harm.' This was by no means certain, of course; it was said to soothe her.

Reich drew the curtains back, and the noise woke Ribot up. He was unshaven and looked very ill; when he saw us, he stared blankly for a moment, then said: 'Ah, gentlemen. I thought you might call.'

I looked into his brain, and what I saw horrified me. It was like a town whose inhabitants have all been massacred and replaced by soldiers. There were no parasites present; they were unnecessary. Ribot had surrendered to the parasites in terror. They had entered his brain and taken over all the habit circuits. When these were all broken, he was virtually helpless, for every act now had to be performed with immense effort, through free-will. We do most of our living through the habit circuits: breathing, eating, digesting, reading, responding to other people. In some cases – an actor, for example – the habit circuits are actually the result of a lifetime of effort. The greater the actor, the more he relies on habit circuits, so that only the supreme peaks of his art are left to his free will. To destroy a man's habit circuits before his eyes is crueller than murdering his wife and children. It is to strip him of everything, to make life as impossible for him as if you had stripped him of his skin. The parasites had done this, then quickly replaced the old habit circuits with new ones. Certain circuits were restored: breathing, speaking, mannerisms (for these were essential to convincing people that he was the same person, and in full possession of his senses). But certain habits were completely eliminated – the habit of thinking deeply, for example. And a new series of responses had been installed. We were 'the enemy', and we aroused in him boundless hatred and disgust. He felt this of his own free will, in a sense; but if he had not chosen to feel it half his circuits would have gone dead again. In other words, having surrendered to the parasites, he remained a ' free man ' in the sense that he was alive and could choose his actions. But it was consciousness *on their terms* – either that, or no consciousness at all. He was as completely a slave as a man with a gun pressed to his head.

So, as we stood around his bed, we did not look at him as avengers. We felt pity and horror. It was like looking at a mutilated corpse.

We did not speak. Four of us held him down – by PK, of course – while Fleishman quickly examined the contents of his brain. It was impossible to tell whether he could be repaired, for it depended so much upon his own strength and courage. All that was certain was that he would have to exert enormous will-power – far more than he had succeeded in exerting against the parasites before he capitulated.

It was no time for long deliberations. Our strength convinced him that he had as much to fear from us as from the parasites. Each one of us entered into the circuits of his brain that controlled his motor mechanisms, and learned their combination. (This is difficult to explain to non-telepaths; but communication with other brains depends upon learning a certain ' combination ' which is their thought wave-length. After this, a degree of remote control is possible.) Fleishman spoke to him gently, telling him that we were still basically his friends, and that we realized the ' brain washing ' was no fault of his. If he would trust us, we would free him from the parasites.

Then we all left. The nurse and porter escorted us down. We thanked the porter, and tipped him in dollars (which were then world currency.) In less than an hour, we were halfway back to Diyarbakir.

Our mental contact with Ribot enabled us to discover what happened when we left. Neither the nurse nor the porter could fully understand how we had forced them to take us to Ribot; they could not believe that it was not of their own free will. So there was no hue and cry. The nurse went back to Ribot and found him awake and apparently unharmed, and decided to say nothing.

As we landed in Diyarbakir, Reich said: 'Seven o'clock. Two hours before he gives his press conference. Let's hope they don't . . .'

He was interrupted by a cry from Fleishman, who had agreed to keep up telepathic contact with Ribot. He said:

'They've found out . . . They're attacking in force.'

I asked: 'What can we do?' I tried to concentrate, to use my knowledge of Ribot's brain to re-establish contact, but there was no result. It was like turning on a radio set when you've forgotten to connect it to the mains. I asked Fleishman:

'Are you still in touch?'

He shook his head. Each of us tried in turn. It was useless.

An hour later, we discovered why. The television news announced that Ribot had committed suicide by leaping from his bedroom window.

Was this a defeat or not? We could not tell. Ribot's suicide prevented him from telling the truth at his press conference and withdrawing his 'confession'. It also prevented him from doing us further damage. On the other hand, if our visit to the hospital was discovered, we would certainly be accused of killing him . . .

As it happened, it was never discovered. Probably the nurse continued to believe that we were just intrusive journalists. She had seen Ribot after we left and he was well. So she said nothing.

At eleven o'clock that morning Reich and I summoned the press to the board room, which had been lent us for that purpose. Fleishman, Reich and the Graus waited on either side of the door, probing everyone who came in. Our caution was rewarded. One of the last men to come into the room was a huge bald-headed man, Kilbride of the *Washington Examiner*. Reich nodded to one of the company guards, who approached Kilbride and asked him if he would mind being searched. He immediately began to protest vehemently and noisily, shouting that it was an indignity. Then suddenly he broke loose and ran towards me, reaching for his inside pocket. I exerted all my mental force, and stopped him short. Three guards hurled themselves on him and dragged him out. They found a Walther automatic pistol in his pocket, with six shots in it and one in the barrel. Kilbride protested that he always carried it for protection, but his action in trying to shoot me had been seen by everyone. (Later, we probed his brain and discovered that the parasites had invaded it while he was drunk the day before – he was well known as an alcoholic.)

This diversion produced a strong atmosphere of expectancy. There were about five hundred reporters present – all the room would hold. The rest watched outside on closed circuit television. Reich, Fleishman and the Grau brothers joined me on the platform – their purpose was actually to scan the hall and make sure there were no more potential assassins – and I read aloud the following statement:

' Our aim today is to warn the people of the earth about a greater menace than they have ever faced. This planet is at present being watched by an enormous number of alien intelligences, whose aim is either to destroy the human race or to enslave it.

' Some months ago, when we were conducting our first archaeological investigations into the Black Mountain at Karatepe, Professor Reich and I became aware that we were in the presence of disturbing forces. We were aware, that is, of a power that actively resisted our efforts to uncover the secret of the mound. We assumed at the time that this power could be in the nature of some psychic field of force established there by long dead inhabitants for the protection of their tombs. Both Reich and myself had long been convinced that such things were possible, and explained, for example, the difficulties of the first excavators of the tomb of Tutankhamen. We were prepared to risk invoking this curse, if this was its nature, and continued our investigations.

'But in recent weeks we have become convinced that we are facing something far more dangerous than a curse. It is our conviction that we have disturbed the sleep of forces that once dominated the earth, and who are determined to dominate it again. These forces are more dangerous than any yet known to the human race because they are invisible, and are capable of attacking the human mind directly. They are able to destroy the sanity of any individual they attack, and to cause suicide. They are also capable of enslaving certain individuals and of using them for their own purposes.

'At the same time, it is our belief that the human race has no cause for panic. Their numbers are small compared to ours, and we have been forewarned. The struggle may be hard, but I think that there is every chance that we shall win.

'I shall now try to summarize what we have succeeded in learning about these mind parasites . . .'

I spoke for about half an hour, and described briefly most of the events that I have recorded here. I told the story of the destruction of our colleagues, and of how Ribot had been made to betray us. Then I explained how, once one became aware of the existence of these parasites, it was possible to destroy them. I went to great trouble to emphasize that these forces were not yet *active*; they were blind and instinctive. It was important to prevent panic. Most of the human race could do nothing whatever about these parasites, and it was best that they should feel fairly confident of ultimate victory. I spent the last quarter of an hour of my talk emphasizing the bright side of things: how, now that man was forewarned, the destruction of the parasites could be only a matter of time.

We concluded the meeting by inviting questions; but most of the reporters were so anxious to get to the nearest tele-screen that the question period was short. Two hours later, the news was on the front page of every newspaper in the world.

To tell the truth, all this bored me. The five of us were explorers preparing to investigate an exciting new world, and it was tiresome to have to waste time on reporters. But we had decided that this was the best way of ensuring our own safety. If we died now, it would alert the whole world. As it was, the best plan of the parasites would be to try to discredit us by allowing everything to proceed normally for a month or so – perhaps even a year or so – until everyone decided it had all been a hoax. By making our announcement now, we had bought time – this, at any rate, was the idea. It would take us a long while to realize that the parasites could out-manoeuvre us on almost every point.

The reason for this should be obvious. We didn't *want* to waste time on the parasites. Imagine a bibliophile who has just received a parcel containing a book he has wanted all his life, and imagine that, before he has opened it, he is interrupted by a bore who insists on talking for hours . . . The parasites may have been the greatest menace ever faced by the human race, but to us, they were the dreariest of bores.

Human beings get so used to their mental limitations, just as the men of three centuries ago got used to the enormous inconvenience of travelling. How would Mozart have felt if, after some exhausting journey lasting a week, someone had told him that the men of the twenty-first century would do it in a quarter of an hour? Well, we were like Mozarts who had been swept forward into the twenty-first century. Those mental journeys which we had once found so exhausting and painful could now be made in a matter of minutes. At last we understood clearly Teilhard de Chardin's remark that man stands on the brink of a new phase in his evolution. For we were now *in* that new phase. The mind was like virgin country, like the promised land of the Israelites. All we had to do was to occupy it . . . and, of course, expel its present inhabitants. So in spite of these anxieties and problems, our mood during these days was one of ecstatic happiness.

As we saw it, we now had two major tasks. The first was to find new 'pupils', others to help us in this fight. The second was to explore the possibility that we could turn this into an *offensive* battle. At present, we could not reach those lower regions of the mind inhabited by the parasites. Yet my night battle with them had taught me that I could call upon a power that came from some very deep source. Could we get close enough to that source to carry the battle into the enemy's camp?

I paid only perfunctory attention to the reactions of the world press. Not surprisingly, most of them were hostile and sceptical. The *World Free Press* of Vienna said openly that the five of us should be placed under close arrest until the whole question of the suicides could be investigated. The London *Daily Express*, on the other hand, suggested that we should be placed in charge of a United Nations War Department, with full powers to combat the parasites by any means we considered effective.

One item disturbed us all. It was an article in the *Berliner Tagblatt* by Felix Hazard. He did not, as we had expected, ridicule the whole business and support Ribot's 'confession'. He seemed to take it for granted that the world was in danger from this new enemy. But if this enemy was capable of 'taking over' individual minds, said Hazard, what guarantee was there that *we* were not slaves of these parasites? We had made this announcement about their existence, but that proved nothing. We *had* to make the announcement out of self-preservation; after Ribot's statement, we were likely to find ourselves facing criminal proceedings . . . The tone of this article was not entirely serious. Hazard seemed to leave open the possibility that he was ridiculing the whole thing with mild satire. Still, the effect was disturbing. There could be no possible doubt in our minds that Hazard was an agent of the enemy.

There was one more matter that needed immediate consideration. So far, reporters had not been allowed into the site at the Black Mountain. But they would obviously have no difficulty in speaking to various workmen and soldiers from the site. This, if possible, had to be forestalled. So Reich and I proposed to escort a selected group of reporters to the site that evening, and we agreed to the presence of television cameras. We gave instructions that the strictest security precautions were to be observed before we arrived; no reporters were to be allowed near the site.

At ten o'clock that evening, fifty reporters were waiting for us in two transport helicopters. The journey to Karatepe took an hour in these cumbrous machines. When we arrived, the whole site had been floodlit. Portable television cameras had been set up ten minutes before we landed.

Our plan seemed foolproof. We would escort the group of reporters down as far as the Abhoth block, which was now fully exposed, and we would use our PK powers to create an atmosphere of oppression and tension. Then we would deliberately pick on the most nervous and susceptible members of the group, and try to induce total panic in them. This, of course, was our reason for failing to mention our PK powers in the earlier interview. We realized that they could, in fact, be used for ' framing ' the parasites.

We reckoned without the parasites. Just before landing, I noticed that the reporters in the other helicopter appeared to be singing. This seemed odd. We presumed that they had been drinking heavily. The Graus, Fleishman, Reich and myself were in the other helicopter. Then, as soon as we landed, we sensed the presence of parasites, and understood what was happening. They were reversing their usual method. Instead of sucking energy from their victims, they were *giving* energy. Many of these men were heavy drinkers and, like most reporters, not particularly intelligent. Because of their habit patterns, this ' gift ' of mental energy had upon them much the same effect as drink. As soon as the reporters from our helicopter joined the others, they were infected by the same party spirit. I heard the television commentator saying: ' Well, these boys certainly don't seem worried about the parasites. They seem to be treating the whole thing as a joke.'

I told the producer of the programme that there would be some delay, and beckoned the others over to a foreman's hut on the far side of the digging. We locked the door, and concentrated on finding out what could be done. The link between us was easily established, and we were able to enter the brains of some of the reporters. At first, it was difficult to discover what was happening; we had never come across anything like this before. Then, luckily, we came upon a reporter whose wave-length was identical with that of Ribot. This enabled us to conduct a closer exploration into his cerebral processes. The brain has about a dozen major pleasure circuits, the most familiar being the sexual, the emotional and the social. There is also an intellectual pleasure circuit, and a higher-intellectual circuit, connected with man's powers of self-control and self-conquest. Finally, there are five circuits that are almost entirely undeveloped in human beings, connected with the energies that we call poetical, religious or mystical.

The parasites were boosting the energy of the social and emtional circuits in most of these men. The fact that there were fifty of them did the rest: the ' crowd ' mechanism amplified their pleasure.

All five of us concentrated on the reporter we were examining. We had no difficulty in breaking the circuit and reducing him to a sudden state of depression. But as soon as we withdrew the pressure, he recovered.

We tried a direct attack on the parasites. It was hopeless. They were beyond our reach, and determined to stay beyond it. We had a feeling that the energy we directed against them was completely wasted, and that they were mocking us.

It was a dangerous situation. We decided that we would have to rely entirely on PK powers to keep the situation in hand. This meant working in close proximity to the reporters.

Someone banged on the door of our hut and shouted 'Hey, how much longer you gonna keep us waiting?' So we went out, and said we were now ready.

I went ahead with Reich. The reporters followed us, laughing cheerfully, and the voice of the television commentator went on continually in the background. Walking at the back of the crowd, Fleishman and the Grau brothers concentrated on this television commentary. We heard the man say in a worried voice: 'Well, everybody seems very light-hearted, but I can't help wondering if it's genuine. There's a strange kind of tension here tonight . . .' At this, the reporters all began to laugh. And now the five of us linked our wills in series, and exerted a pressure of insecurity and vague fear. Immediately, the laughter stopped. I said aloud: 'Don't worry. The air at this depth isn't as pure as it might be. But it's not poisonous.'

The tunnel was seven feet high, and sloped at an angle of about twenty degrees. A hundred yards down, we were all able to climb into a number of small railway wagons. During the ten mile journey, nothing was audible above the rattle of the wheels. There was no need to exert any pressure to lower their spirits as we went downwards. The tunnel was roughly corkscrew-shaped – the alternative would have been to place its entrance several miles from the Black Mountain, and set up another site, which would have doubled our security problem. Every time the trucks lurched around a bend, we felt the wave of alarm that rose from them. They were also afraid that the vibrations of the trucks might collapse part of the tunnel.

It took nearly half an hour to get down to the Abhoth

block. This in itself was an impressive enough sight; its immense, grey-black sides towered above us like a cliff.

Now we deliberately created an atmosphere of oppression. It would have been far better if we could have allowed their imaginations to work, and merely stimulated them with a touch of fear. But the parasites were pouring energy into them, and it was necessary for us to paralyse the parts of their brains that would respond. So we exerted a dead weight of fear and distaste. The television commentator was obviously embarrassed to go on talking in the oppressive silence; he was speaking into his microphone in a whisper. ' There's an unpleasant, suffocating feeling down here. It could be the air.'

Then the parasites began to attack. Not in force, this time, but in ones and twos. Their purpose was obviously to harass us, to make us lose our grip. As soon as we turned our attention to fighting them, the atmosphere lightened; everybody became more cheerful. It was a frustrating experience, for there was little that could be done. In small numbers, they were almost invulnerable. It was like fighting shadows. The best thing was to ignore them, but this was as difficult as to ignore a mongrel dog snapping at your ankles.

And then the idea came to all of us simultaneously: at least, we were so linked that it is impossible to say who thought of it first. We looked at the Abhoth block, and at the ceiling that was some thirty feet above it. It weighed three thousand tons. The Grau brothers had lifted a thirty ton block in the British Museum. We decided that it was worth trying. So after deliberately sending a wave of fear over the reporters, we began to exert our wills in unison to lift the block.

It seemed hopeless, as hopeless as trying to lift it with our bare hands. Then the Grau brothers gave us the clue. Instead of exerting the effort in unison, they exerted it *alternately*, at first slowly, then with increasing speed. We understood what they were doing, and joined in. The moment we had grasped

140

the trick, it became absurdly easy. The power that five of us generated in this way was immense, enough to have lifted the two miles of earth above us. The block suddenly floated clear of the ground, and moved up to the ceiling. The lights flickered as it brushed a power cable. There was an immediate panic, and some of the idiots ran under the block, or were pushed under. We moved it sideways, and immediately plunged the place into darkness as the block ripped the power cable. The end of the cable trailed on the ground, and we heard a man give a throaty scream as he stumbled on it. The smell of charred flesh filled the chamber and made us all feel sick.

It was important not to panic. One of us had to disengage his will and push the reporters to the edge of the chamber, so the block could be lowered without delay. This was difficult, since our wills were 'locked' together upholding the block. We were, so to speak, in parallel instead of in series, sustaining the block with a five-fold alternation.

This was the moment the parasites chose to attack in force. They had us helpless, of course. The situation would have been funny if it had not been so dangerous, and if it had not already cost a life.

It was Reich who said: 'Could we atomize it?' For a moment, in the confusion, we failed to understand him – the parasites were surrounding us like an army of shadows. Then, as we saw what he meant, we knew it was the only hope. The power we were exerting was enough to lift a thousand blocks of this size: would it be enough to destroy this one? We tried it, gripping the block mentally and exerting a crushing pressure on it. We increased the rate of alternations automatically, and the exhilaration was so great that we scarcely noticed the pressure of the parasites around us. Then we felt it grind and crumble like an enormous piece of chalk held in a vice. In a few seconds, it was a great block of fine powder we were holding in the air. In this form, it could be forced into the tunnel. This we did, at such a pace that the draught sucked us back towards the tunnel, and the air filled for a while with dust.

The moment the block was out of the way, we used the accumulated will-power to lash out at the parasites, with the impatience of a man striking at a flea. The result was satisfying; again, they had not time to retreat, and we had the sensation of cutting into them like a flame-thrower into dead leaves. Then Reich disengaged his will and picked up the end of the power cable, which he fused to the broken end. The lights came on, and showed us utter confusion. The ' social circuit ' had been snapped in all of them; each man felt himself totally alone, and terrified. The air was full of black dust that made us all choke. (We had to allow it to settle in the tunnel before we could drive it upwards, in order to allow clean air to flow in above it.) The remains of the dead man were stuck to the power cable above us, and still produced a charring smell. We were all black in the face, like coal miners. The atmosphere of panic was terrifying. Each one of them believed that he would never see the surface again.

We were able to still the panic by again linking in series. Then we ordered them to form into a double line, and return to the trucks. Reich concentrated on the three television men, making sure that they started their cameras again. (The power cut had affected them, of course.) Meanwhile, the rest of us cleared the dust out of the tunnel, and sent it slowly up to the surface, where it rose into the sky – luckily it was a dark night – and was allowed to settle over a wide area.

When we came out into the air, we knew that we had won a considerable victory over the parasites – mainly by accident. They had not given up, of course. They were still pouring energy into the reporters as we came to the surface. We were able to block this completely. But obviously we would be unable to do so when they separated. Still, the whole world had seen what had happened over the television cameras, and had seen the disappearance of the block. Whatever the reporters wrote hardly mattered. Besides, there was another factor. This artificial boosting of their social and emotional circuits would inevitably produce a reaction of fatigue, a kind of hangover. They could not be kept in this state of semi-intoxication forever. The reaction should serve us well.

It was after midnight when the five of us ate a meal together. It was in a special room that A.I.U. had provided for us. We had decided that, from now on, the five of us had to stay together, by day and night. Singly, we had a certain strength, but together, this strength was multiplied by a thousand, as we had demonstrated that evening.

We did not deceive ourselves into believing that we were invulnerable. We were, perhaps, safe from direct attack from the parasites. But they knew how to use other men against us, and this was the real danger.

When we saw the newspapers the next morning, it was difficult not to congratulate ourselves on a major victory. Since almost everyone in the world had been watching their television screens, it was as if everyone had been present when the Abhoth block vanished. We thought that a few of the newspapers would suspect fraud – after all, what we had done was no more than a glorified conjuring trick – but no one did. There were plenty of hysterical attacks on us, but they were attacks on our stupidity in releasing these ' terrifying forces '. Everyone assumed that the ' Tsathogguans ' – it was a Lovecraft expert in the States who was responsible for the name – had destroyed the block to prevent us from learning more of their secrets. What terrified everyone was that if they could destroy a three thousand ton block, they could destroy a modern city just as easily. This fear was increased later in the day when scientists detected the layer of basalt dust covering the scrub for miles around the site, and deduced correctly that the block had been somehow disintegrated. They were baffled. It would, of course, have been possible to disintegrate the block using an atomic blaster, but the resultant release of energy would have destroyed everyone in the underground chamber; they could not understand how it had been done without even raising the temperature of the chamber.

Gunnar Fangen, the president of the United Nations, sent us a message asking what steps we thought he should take against the parasites. Did we think it would help if Kadath was destroyed by atomic mines? Had we any idea of what weapons might be effective against them? We sent him a message asking him to come and see us, which he did forty-eight hours later.

Meanwhile, A.I.U. was facing a problem of its own. The publicity of course, was highly gratifying; but while hundreds of reporters waited outside, they were in a state of siege, and business came to a standstill. It was important that we find ourselves a new headquarters. For this reason, I spoke directly to the President of the United States, Lloyd C. Melville, asking him if he could find us a high security area where we would be guaranteed privacy. He acted quickly, and within an hour notified us that we could move to the U.S. Rocket Base 91, at Saratoga Springs, New York State. We moved there the following day, October 17th.

Our new base had many advantages. We still had a list of a dozen men in America whom we had intended to ' initiate ' into our secret in due course; their names had been supplied by Reimizov and Spencefield of Yale. Five of them were in New York State. We asked President Melville if he would ask these men to meet us on our arrival at Base 91. The men were Oliver Fleming and Merril Philips of the Psychological Laboratory of Columbia, Russell Holcroft of Syracuse University, and Edward Leaf and Viktor Ebner of the Albany Research Institute.

The evening before we left A.I.U., Fleishman made a television appearance, recorded at A.I.U., in which he again emphasized that earth had no cause for panic. He did not believe that the parasites were strong enough to do any real damage to the human race. It was our business to try to make sure they never became strong enough.

For us, this ' public ' side of our work was the least important; in fact, it was a tiresome irrelevancy. We wanted to get down to the real business of exploring our own strength and that of the parasites.

A.I.U. organized a fast rocket to take us to Base 91, and we were there within an hour. Our arrival was announced on television the same afternoon. The President made a personal appearance to explain his reasons for allowing us into Base 91 (which was the United States' maximum security area – a joke said it was easier for a camel to pass through the eye of a needle than to get into Base 91). He said that our safety was a matter of world importance, and that any attempt by reporters to contact us would be treated as a breach of security regulations, and dealt with as such. This certainly solved one of our major problems; from that time onward, we could move about without being followed by a dozen helicopters.

Base 91 was hardly comfortable compared with the directors' block at A.I.U. Our quarters consisted of a nissen hut that had been constructed in the twenty-four hours before our arrival; it was little more than a well-furnished barrack room.

The five men were waiting to meet us when we arrived – Fleming, Philips, Holcroft, Leaf and Ebner. All were under forty. Holcroft hardly looked like a scientist, being over six feet tall with pink cheeks and very blue eyes : I felt some misgivings on seeing him. The others struck me as first-rate men : intelligent, self-controlled, and with a sense of humour. We all had tea with the O.I.C. of the base and the chief security officer. Both these men seemed to me typical soldiers; intelligent enough, but somehow literal-minded. (The security officer wanted to know what measures he could take against Tsathogguan spies.) I decided to try to make them understand precisely what we were up against; not an enemy who attacked you from in front or behind, but one who was *already inside us all.* They looked baffled until General Winslow, the O.I.C., said ' I suppose you mean you

145

could compare these creatures to germs that get into the bloodstream?' I said that indeed you could, and from then on I had a feeling that they were altogether happier about the idea, although the security officer was now thinking in terms of disinfectant.

After tea, we took the five new ' recruits ' back to the hut. I read in the security officer's mind that there were a number of vibration microphones concealed under the concrete floor of our hut – placed there on his own orders – so as soon as we moved in, I located them and destroyed them. They were, of course, set in the concrete itself an inch deep, so it should have been theoretically impossible to destroy them without drilling into the concrete. Whenever I saw the security officer over the next week, I caught him looking at me in an odd way.

We spent the evening explaining the situation to our five ' recruits '. First of all, they were given photostated copies of the *Historical Reflections* to read. Then I told them briefly my own story. While I did so, it was tape recorded, so that it could be played back later if they still had questions. I quote here from the last five minutes of that tape recording, since it states clearly the nature of the problems we faced:

' So we suspect that these things can be combated by a human being with a basic training in phenomenology. We also know that their chief power seems to lie in their ability to unbalance the mind. (I had already confessed that the destruction of the Abhoth block was our doing.) This means that we have to learn how to resist them at every mental level.

' But this in itself raises a new problem, which we must solve as quickly as possible. We know so little about the human soul. We do not know what happens when a man is born and when he dies. We do not understand man's relation to space and time.

' The great vision of the nineteenth century romantics was of " men like gods ". We now know that this is within the bounds of possibility. Man's potential powers are so immense

146

that we cannot begin to grasp them. To be god-like means to be in *control* of things instead of being a victim of circumstance. But it must be emphasized that there can be no ultimate control while there are great unanswered questions. If a man walks with his face turned to the sky, it is easy to trip him up. While we do not understand the foundations of our being, these parasites could be planning to attack these foundations and destroy us. For all I know, these parasites are as ignorant as we are about these questions. But we cannot risk making that assumption. We have got to know the secrets of death and of space and time. This is our only guarantee of winning this fight.'

To my surprise – and great pleasure – Holcroft turned out to be one of the best pupils I'd ever had. That look of babyish innocence was, in a way, a true guide to his nature. He had been brought up in the country by two maiden aunts who adored him, and had done well in science at school. He was naturally generous and sunny and un-neurotic, so this fortunate background allowed him to preserve these qualities. As an experimental psychologist, he was not brilliant: he lacked the kind of nervous drive that makes a first-rate scientist. But what was far more important is that he had a natural, instinctive adjustment to nature. He had a kind of spiritual radar that meant that he made fairly light work of the business of living.

So in a way, he *already knew* everything I told him. It instantly made sense to him. The others understood it intellectually, and digested it slowly, like a python digesting a rat, in a state of intellectual excitement. Holcroft knew it all instinctively.

Now this was far more important than it sounds. For Reich and Fleishman and myself and the Graus were also intellectuals. We could not get out of the habit of trying to use the intellect to explore the world of the mind, and this tended to waste time – like an army commanded by a general who refuses to act without making out documents in triplicate and consulting headquarters about everything. Holcroft was a kind of ' medium '; not a spirit medium, although this is closely related. His sphere was not the 'spirit' but the instincts. On that first evening, we were able to ' key him in' to our telepathic circle; his inner ear was naturally attuned to us. And a new hope sprang up among the five of us. Could this man dive deeper into the mind than we could? Could he give us some idea of what the parasites were up to?

For the next two or three days, we spent most of the time in our hut, teaching our new pupils all we knew. Our telepathic powers made this easy. But we also came to recognize that we had overlooked one of the most important problems of phenomenology. When you teach a man that he has been completely mistaken about his own nature all his life, it is as unsettling as suddenly giving him a million pounds. Or it is like taking a sexually frustrated man, and giving him the run of a harem. He suddenly discovers that he can turn on moods of poetry like a tap, that he can heat up his emotions to a kind of incandescence. He realizes, with a shock, that he has been handed the key to *greatness*: that all the world's so-called ' great men ' were men who had a mere glimmering of these powers which he now possesses in abundance. But he has spent all his life taking a relatively modest view of himself. His old personality has achieved a certain density through thirty or forty years of habit. It refuses to wither away overnight. But the new personality is also exceptionally powerful. He becomes a battle ground of two personalities. And he wastes an enormous amount of energy in all this confusion.

Holcroft, as I have said, was an excellent pupil; but the other four had far more strongly developed personalities. And they had no real feeling of danger or urgency: after all, the rest of us had survived an attack from the parasites, so why shouldn't they?

I am not blaming these four men. It was almost inevitable.

Every university faces a version of this same problem: students who find their new life so fascinating that they don't want to waste it in hard work.

It cost the five of us a considerable mental effort to prevent Fleming, Philips, Leaf and Ebner from throwing all discipline to the winds. We had to watch them constantly. These new ideas were a powerful intoxicant; their minds were so stimulated that they wanted to splash around like happy schoolboys in a river. While they should have been reading Husserl or Merleau Ponty, they would start to remember scenes of childhood or past love affairs. Ebner was a music lover who knew all the operas of Wagner by heart, and as soon as he was left to himself, he would begin to hum some theme from the Ring, and immediately sink into a passive ecstasy. Philips was something of a Don Juan, and would recall past conquests until the atmosphere vibrated with a sexual excitement that the rest of us found distracting. In defence of Philips, I should say that his sexual adventures had always been a search for something he never found; now he had suddenly found it, and he couldn't stop himself from holding constant post mortems on the past.

On the third day after our arrival at Base 91, Holcroft came over to talk to me. He said:

'I've got a feeling that we're making fools of ourselves.'

I asked with foreboding what he meant.

'I don't quite know. But when I practise trying to pick up their wavelength ' (he meant the parasites) ' I get a feeling of great activity. They're up to something.'

It was maddeningly frustrating. We possessed the great secret; we had warned the world. And yet, in a fundamental sense, we were as ignorant as ever. Who were these creatures? Where did they come from? What was their ultimate aim? Were they really intelligent, or were they as unintelligent as the maggots in a piece of cheese?

We asked ourselves these questions often enough, and had arrived at a few tentative answers. Human intelligence is a

149

function of man's evolutionary urge; the scientist and the philosopher hunger for truth because they are tired of being merely human. Now, was it possible that these creatures were intelligent in the same way? Since they were our enemies, it was hard to believe. But history has taught us that intelligence is no guarantee of benevolence. At all events, *if* they were intelligent, perhaps we might propose a truce? Again, *if* they were intelligent, perhaps they might realize that they were beaten.

But were they beaten?

As soon as Holcroft had spoken to me about his suspicions, I called the others together. It was after breakfast, on a clear, bright morning, with plenty of warmth in the air. A few hundred yards away, a group of airmen in white gym tunics were drilling, and we could hear the shout of the sergeant's voice.

I explained my fears, and said that I thought we would have to make an attempt to learn something more about the parasites. We asked our four ' pupils ' to make an effort to establish telepathic link with us. This was going to be a dangerous operation, and we needed all the support we could get. After half an hour of practice, Leaf suddenly announced that he was getting us clearly. The others had exhausted themselves in the effort to reach us, so we told them to forget it, and relax. We did not say what was in our minds: that in the event of an attack from the parasites, they would be in the greatest danger, since they had had so little practice in using their mental powers.

We drew the blinds, locked the doors, and all sat and concentrated hard. I had become so used to this operation that I did it almost automatically. The first step was identical with the one I take when I wish to fall asleep; complete dismissal of the outside world, forgetfulness of my body. Within seconds, I was plunging downwards into the darkness of my own mind. The next step took some practice. I had to detach myself from my ordinary physical personality. The intelligent part of me had to remain wide awake, and move down into this world of dreams and memories.

This operation is, in a way, similar to what happens if you are having a nightmare, and you tell yourself: 'This is only a dream; I am asleep in my bed; I must wake up.' Your daylight self is present, but it is bewildered in its world of phantasmagoria. I soon found that I could descend through the layer of dreams retaining full consciousness – a difficult trick, since human beings use the body as a kind of reflector of consciousness. It is a strange, silent world, the dream layer of the mind, one feels literally like swimming under the sea. For a beginner, this can be the most dangerous part of the experience. The body acts as an anchor on the mind. In one of his poems, Yeats thanks God that he 'has body and its stupidity' to rescue him from his nightmares. The body acts as a great weight on our thoughts, and prevents them from floating all over the place. It is rather like being on the moon, and only weighing a few pounds. If you take an ordinary step, you go flying through the air like a balloon. Thoughts also gain this demonic energy when freed of the body's gravity. If the thinker happens to be a morbid sort of person, his thoughts immediately become terrifying devils. And unless he happens to know that these are *his* thoughts, and that they have no existence apart from him, he may become panic-stricken and make everything ten times worse. It is like a man in an aeroplane going into a steep dive, and failing to realize that he is unconsciously pushing the joystick forward.

As I bumped gently downwards through my dreams and memories, I took care to remain passive, to ignore them. If I made the mistake of concentrating on any one of them, it would instantly expand and become a universe of its own. For example, I encountered the smell of a pipe tobacco called Ginger Tom that my grandfather used to smoke. It had been so long since I had remembered it that I paused and allowed my interest to be drawn towards it. Immed-

151

iately, I became aware of my grandfather, and of the back garden of his Lincolnshire cottage. In fact, I was *in* the back garden, and it was re-created in a minute detail that, under different circumstances, would have convinced me of its reality. I made a determined effort to dismiss it, and in a moment was again sinking down into the warm darkness.

This darkness is full of life, and it is not simply a reflection of the life of the body. It is the life that swarms like electricity throughout the universe. So the lower regions of the mind have been referred to as the ' nursery '. There is an intensely alive feeling of warmth and innocence; it is a world of children without bodies.

Below the ' nursery ', there is an emptiness that is like the emptiness of interstellar space, a sort of nothingness. This is a particularly terrifying region where it is easy to lose your bearings. In all my early experiments, I always fell asleep in this region and woke up many hours later. There is nothing to reflect back one's feeling of individuality, or even of existence, so that a single moment's inattention loses the thread of consciousness.

This was as far as I could go. Even then, I had to allow myself to rise periodically to the nursery region, to concentrate my attention.

During all this time, our brains remained in telepathic contact. This is not to say that all seven of us were swimming side by side, so to speak. Each was alone; it was the brains that maintained contact. All this meant was that we were able to help one another by a kind of remote control. If I had fallen asleep when I paused in my grandmother's garden, the others could have wakened me. If one of us was attacked, we would all ' wake up ' instantly and unite to repulse the attack. But at that depth, you were on your own.

It was now that my remote contact with Holcroft told me that he was still descending. I was filled with admiration. I had become absolutely weightless at that depth. My cons-

152

ciousness was like a bubble that wanted to rise. I knew there was some 'knack' of getting deeper, but acquiring a knack takes a certain amount of exploration, of practice, and if it is all you can do to remain conscious, this is impossible. Holcroft obviously had the knack already.

There is almost no sense of time in these regions of the mind – it passes and yet it does not pass, if this makes any sense. Since there is no body to get impatient, there is something neutral about its passage. I could tell that there were no parasites anywhere near me, so I simply waited, keeping my attention alert. Soon I gathered that Holcroft was returning. I floated gently back upwards, through the dreams and memories, and came back to physical consciousness about an hour after the experiment had begun. Holcroft was still unconscious It was about ten minutes before he opened his eyes. The colour had left his cheeks, but he was breathing quietly.

He looked at us calmly, and we saw that he had nothing much to tell us. He said:

' I can't understand it. There's almost nothing going on down there. I could almost believe they'd all cleared out.'

' Didn't you see any?'

'No I had a feeling once or twice that there were some around, but very few.'

We all recorded the same experience. It looked hopeful. But none of us felt very happy.

At midday, for the first time in three days, we turned on the television news. And then we found out what the parasites had been doing for the past three days. We learned of Obafeme Gwambe's murder of President Nkumbula of the United States of Africa, and the *coup d'etat* that had made him master of Cape Town and Aden. Then there was an extract from the speech Gwambe made over the radio after the coup. We looked at one another. The voice was oddly expressionless, as if he was repeating something learned by rote, and was too tired to do it justice. ' For too many years

153

now the black man has looked on himself as the white man's inferior. This has got to stop. The black man knows that he is superior to the white man in every way. He is physically stronger, he is more sexually potent, he can do longer hours of brain work without getting tired. The twenty-first century will be the century of the black man . . .' And so on. It was all extremely inflammatory stuff, and Gwambe spoke it with a certain conviction. Yet it was somehow too well controlled to sound absolutely convincing, as if Gwambe were an actor who had recorded his speech after a dozen attempts.

The speech ended with a reference to us: ' The white men have thought up a new way of swindling the blacks. They have invented a lot of bogies called the Sagothuans [Gwambe mispronounced it] who are supposed to be invading the earth. Well, has anybody seen any of these bogies yet? No, because they don't exist. It's another trick of the whites to keep the black man's mind off his grievances.'

Gwambe went on to list the ' right ' of the negro population of earth. Each country with a large negro population was to hand over a part of its territory to its negro citizens, and allow them an independent government. America was to hand over the states of Texas and California. England was to hand over its southern counties, including London. The negroes of Europe were to be given a country of their own – either Italy, Poland or Austria.

These details, of course, bothered no one; they were obviously bluff. What *did* bother us was that Gwambe was obviously under the control of the mind parasites. And we now knew enough of the parasites to know that underrating them was the most dangerous of mistakes.

We understood their policy immediately; it was, after all, the policy they had pursued with such success for two centuries now: keeping mankind distracted with war. For two centuries, mankind had laboured to change its state of consciousness for something more intense. For two centuries, the parasites had given them other things to think about.

154

We sat and talked late into the night. This new development obviously called for immediate action – but *what* action? We all had a strange sense of foreboding. At three in the morning we went to bed. At five, Holcroft woke us, and said: ' They're planning something – I can feel it. I think we'd better get out of this place.'

' Where to?'

It was Reich who answered the question.

' To Washington. I think we'd all better go and talk to the president.'

'What good would that do?'

Reich said: ' I don't know. But I have a feeling that we're wasting time while we're sitting here.'

There was no point in delaying. Although there was still an hour to dawn, we went to the helicopter that the United States government had placed at our service. By daylight, we saw the long, straight avenues of Washington below us. We brought it down gently in the street outside the White House. The soldier on duty at the gate came running over, his atom gun raised. He was a young man, and it was not difficult to convince him that he had better fetch his superior officer, while we moved the helicopter on to the White House lawn. This was one of the pleasantest advantages of our powers: the ordinary obstacles of officialdom vanished.

We gave the officer a message for the president, and then went for a walk to find coffee. To casual passers-by, the eleven of us probably looked like a business delegation. We found a big, glass-plated restaurant, and occupied two tables overlooking the street. As we sat there, I looked into Ebner's mind. He felt my probing, and smiled at me. He said:

' It's funny. I ought to be thinking about the danger that confronts the human race, and the city of my birth – I was born in Washington. Instead of that, I feel a kind of contempt for these people wandering by in the street. They're all asleep. It doesn't really seem to matter much what happens to them . . .'

155

Reich said, smiling: 'Don't forget you were one of them a week ago.'

I telephoned the White House, and discovered that we had been invited to breakfast with the president at nine o'clock. As we walked back through the morning crowds on their way to work, we suddenly felt a faint tremor in the pavements. We looked at one another, and Ebner said: 'Earthquake?'

Reich said: 'No. An explosion.'

We quickened our step, and arrived back at the White House at 8.45. I asked the officer who came to meet us if he'd heard any news of an explosion. He shook his head. 'What explosion?'

We found out twenty minutes later, just after we had sat down to breakfast. The president was called out. When he came back, his face was bloodless, and his voice was trembling. He said: 'Gentlemen, Base 91 was destroyed by an explosion half an hour ago.' None of us spoke, but the same thought came to all of us: How long would it be before the parasites caught up with us?

Both Reich and Holcroft have written detailed accounts of that interview with the president, so I shall confine myself to a brief outline of what happened. We saw that he was on the point of collapse, and calmed him by the methods we had now used so often. Melville was not a strong-minded man. He was an excellent peace-time president, with a fine grasp of administration, but not the man to cope with a world crisis. We discovered that he had been so shaken by the news that he had forgotten to ring army headquarters to order America's full defence system to come into action. He was soon persuaded to remedy this, and we were glad to learn that the new high speed particle radar could guarantee the interception of an atomic missile travelling at a mile a second.

Melville was inclined to cling to the hope that the explosion at Base 91 was due to some kind of accident, perhaps to the Mars rocket that was being constructed there. (Its energy units packed enough power to destroy half New York State.) We told him brutally that there was no chance of this. The explosion was the work of the parasites, and they had almost certainly used Gwambe as their instrument. He said that, in that case, America was committed to a full-scale atomic war with Africa. We pointed out that this was not necessarily so. The explosion was aimed at killing us. It had been a throw of the dice that had failed because of chance – and Holcroft's intuition of danger. Gwambe would not have another chance to use this method. So in the meantime, Melville could pretend to believe that the explosion was due to the Mars rocket. But one thing was obviously of immense importance: that we should get together the largest possible number of intelligent men, capable of grasping the problem of the mind parasites, and of training them into a kind of army. If we could get enough men capable of psychokinesis, we might be able to destroy Gwambe's rebellion before it had time to spread. In the meantime, we had to find a place where we could work undisturbed.

The task of providing the president with the moral courage and energy to meet the crisis occupied us for most of the morning. Melville had to appear on television and state that he believed the explosion to have been an accident. (It had destroyed an area with a thirty mile radius – it was no wonder we felt it in Washington.) This did a lot to soothe the nation's nerves. Then the whole American defence system had to be elaborately checked, and a secret message sent to Gwambe warning him that there would be instant reprisals in the event of any further explosions. We decided that it would be better to announce that we were still alive. It was almost impossible to keep this from the parasites. On the other hand, the announcement of our death might cause widespread despair, since millions of people now looked to us for leadership.

But when we sat together for an early lunch, there was a heavy atmosphere of gloom. It seemed impossible that we could win. The only hope was to admit another hundred or so men into our circle of ' initiates ', and then try to destroy Gwambe by the same methods we had used against Georges Ribot. But in all probability we would be under constant observation from the parasites. There was nothing to stop them from taking over other leaders as they had taken over Gwambe. In fact, they could even take over Melville! It was no use thinking about making Melville himself an ' initiate '. Like ninety-five per cent of the human race, he would never be capable of grasping the problem. We were in constant danger. Even as we walked through the streets, the parasites might take over some passer-by, and hurl him at us like a missile. And one passer-by with an atomic pistol could make short work of us.

It was Reich who said:

' It's a pity we can't simply move to another planet and start another race.'

It was not intended to be a serious observation. We knew that no planet in the solar system was habitable; in any case, earth had no space ship capable of carrying human beings the fifty million miles to Mars.

And yet . . . would this not be the answer to the security problem? America *did* have several rockets capable of carrying five hundred people to the moon. And then there were the three satellite stations that were in orbit round the earth. While we remained on earth we were in constant danger from the parasites. Alone in outer space, there would be no danger.

Yes, that was obviously the answer. Immediately after lunch, Reich, Fleishman and I went to the president and explained our idea. If the parasites succeeded in destroying us, then the earth was lost anyway. Having won that battle, they would ruthlessly exterminate everyone who tried to re-discover our secret. The best hope for the earth lay in allowing about fifty of us to embark in a moon rocket, and spend

158

the next few weeks on one of the satellites, or cruising around between earth and the moon. In that time, we might be strong enough to challenge the parasites. If not, then the fifty of us would split up into teaching groups, and each group would take another fifty men into space. We would finally create an army capable of taking over a country.

It has been suggested by one historian that we 'took over' President Melville as the parasites had taken over Gwambe, and forced him to agree to everything we asked. Such a course would, of course, have been justifiable in the crisis; but it was unnecessary for us to take it. Melville was glad enough to do whatever we suggested; the crisis terrified him.

I have said that Spencefield and Remizov had provided us with a list of a dozen men who could be admitted to our circle. We had only covered half this list. Moreover, Holcroft, Ebner and the rest had a number of suggestions of their own. The result was that by late afternoon, we had spoken to some thirty men, all of whom agreed to join us. The US air force collaborated with us in getting them to Washington, and by eight the following morning our group had swelled to thirty-nine members. It should have been forty-one; but the plane bringing two psychologists from Los Angeles crashed over the Grand Canyon. We never discovered the reason for the accident, but it was not difficult to guess.

The president had arranged that we could leave earth the following afternoon from the rocket port at Annapolis. In the meantime, we put our twenty-eight pupils through a high-speed course in phenomenology. We discovered that practice was making us perfect or very nearly so. Perhaps the general atmosphere of crisis also helped. (It had certainly produced an amazing change in Merril, Philips, Leaf, and Ebner.) Before the day was over, we actually had one of our new recruits producing slight PK effects on a piece of cigarette ash.

Still the feeling of foreboding was on us. It was a highly

unpleasant sensation – a feeling that we were menaced from the outside *and* the inside. Against any individual enemy we would have felt confident. But it was frustrating to realize that the parasites might use any one of several billions of people against us. It produced a ' needle in a haystack ' feeling of hopelessness. I must also admit that we kept a close check on the president during all the time we were in Washington; it would have been so easy for the parasites to take over his brain circuits.

Meanwhile, Gwambe's success in Africa was startling. When the United Nations issued a warning to him, he simply used it for propaganda purposes – the white men trying to bully the blacks. And the speed with which his revolt spread made it very clear that the parasites had made Africa the scene of a mass operation of mind-invasion. Without consulting their troops, negro generals declared their allegiance to Gwambe. It took Gwambe only about three days to become virtually the master of the United States of Africa.

The whole of that night before we left earth, I lay awake thinking. I had found that I now needed only a few hours' sleep a night. If I allowed myself to oversleep, the result was a weakening of my mental powers, of my control over my own consciousness. But I now felt that I had to come to grips with a problem that teased and tormented me. I had a feeling that I was overlooking something important.

This was a feeling that had been with me vaguely ever since that night when the parasites destroyed all but five of us. It seemed that, in a sense, we had been at a standstill ever since then. Oh, we had won various minor battles against them – and yet there was still a feeling that our major achievements were over. This seemed stranger still since they had apparently left us alone since the night of the battle.

Animals are very nearly machines; they live on reflex and habit. Human beings are also very largely machines, but we also possess a degree of consciousness, which means, in essence, freedom from habit, the ability to do something new and original. Now I had the frustrating feeling that the 'something' I was overlooking was one of the thousands of habits that we still take for granted. I was struggling for greater control of my consciousness, but I was overlooking some deep-rooted habits that stood in the way of real control.

Let me try to make this point clear. What bothered me was connected with the tremendous rush of vital energy with which I had defeated the parasites. In spite of all my efforts to grasp its source, it still evaded me. Now most human beings discover that sudden emergencies arouse inner-powers of which they were not aware. A war, for example, may turn a hypochondriac into a hero. This is because the vitality of most people is controlled by subconscious forces of which they are not aware. But I *was* aware of these forces. I could descend into my own mind like an engineer into the machinery of a ship. And yet I could not get to that source of real inner power. Why? The emergency of my battle with the parasites had enabled me to call on these tremendous energies. There was something unreasonable about this failure to get down to the root of my vital powers.

All that night, I wrestled with the problem; I tried to descend deeper and deeper into my own mind. It was useless. There seemed to be some invisible obstacle – or perhaps it was simply my own weakness and lack of concentration. The parasites seemed to have nothing to do with it; I didn't see a single one.

At dawn I felt tired, but I went with Reich, Holcroft and the Graus to the Annapolis rocket base to make a final check. It was as well we did. We interviewed the whole team who had prepared our rocket, on the pretext of asking them routine questions. They all seemed completely honest and friendly. We asked them how the work had gone, and they said that it had been a smooth routine job with no hitches. But Holcroft, who had been watching us without saying anything, suddenly asked:

F

'Is there a member of your team who isn't present?'

Colonel Massey, who was in charge of the team, shook his head. 'All the engineers are present.'

Holcroft persisted:

'But is there anyone apart from the engineers?'

'Only one man – but he's not important. Kellerman, Lieutenant Costa's assistant. He had an appointment with the psychiatrist this morning.'

Costa was the man whose chief task was the programming of the electronic brain that co-ordinated the workings of the rocket: fuel, temperature, air control, and so on.

I said casually: 'I know it isn't important, but we'd like to see him. Just a matter of routine.'

'But Lieutenant Costa knows far more about the robot than Kellerman does. He can answer any queries.'

'All the same, we'd like to see him.'

So a call was put through to the base psychiatrist. He said that Kellerman had left him half an hour before. A check with the guard house revealed that Kellerman had gone out on a motor cycle twenty minutes ago. Costa said awkwardly:

'He has a girl-friend on the university campus, and I sometimes let him ride over to take a coffee break with her. I suppose that's where he's gone.'

Reich said casually:

'I'd be glad if you'd send someone over there to fetch him back. In the meantime, would you check all the circuits of the robot brain?'

An hour later, the check had revealed that the brain was in perfect order. But the orderly who had been sent to the university returned without Kellerman. No one had seen him. Costa said: 'Well, he's probably gone off into town to do some shopping. It's a breach of regulations, of course, but I suppose he thought we wouldn't notice on a busy morning . . .'

162

Colonel Massey tried to change the subject, but Reich said:

'I'm sorry Colonel, but we don't intend to leave in this rocket until we've spoken to Kellerman. Would you mind putting out a general call for him?'

They obviously thought us mad and boorish, but they had no alternative but to agree. So a dozen military police cars were sent out, and all the police in the area were alerted. Then a check at the local helicopter terminal revealed that a man of Kellerman's description had taken a plane for Washington several hours ago. The hunt immediately spread to Washington, and the police there were alerted, too.

Kellerman was finally picked up at three-thirty in the afternoon – an hour after we were supposed to have blasted off. He had taken a return trip back from Washington, and was recognized at the local helicopter terminal. He protested that he had slipped off to buy his girl-friend an engagement ring, and thought no one would notice. But as soon as we saw him, we knew our precaution had been justified. He was a curious kind of split personality; a whole area of his personality was completely immature. The parasites had taken advantage of this. There had been no need to take over his brain; the alteration of a few minor circuits had been all that was necessary. His schoolboyish desire to feel important did the rest. It was the same kind of mechanism that sometimes makes juvenile delinquents derail trains for the fun of it: a desire to join the adult world by doing something that has adult consequences.

Once we had Kellerman, there was no difficulty in bullying the truth out of him. He had made some minute adjustments to the temperature controls of the ship, so that the temperature would increase very slightly in outer space – too slightly for us to notice. But this change would cause an automatic adjustment on the part of the robot. This adjustment would affect the braking mechanism of the ship, so that when we approached the satellite, our speed would be far too great;

163

we would smash through the satellite, destroying ourselves and it. The ordinary circuit checks had naturally failed to reveal this: after all, an electronic brain has some billions of possible circuits, and a ' check ' only consists in making sure that its main junctions are responsive.

We left Kellerman to his fate – I understood he was later court-martialled and shot – and blasted off finally at four-thirty. By six o'clock we were doing four thousand miles an hour in the direction of the moon. The gravitational mechanism of the ship was of the old type: the floor was a magnet, and we wore special clothing that was attracted towards it, so that we appeared to have normal weight. The consequence was that we all experienced space dizziness for the first two hours.

When we felt normal, we gathered in the dining-room, and Reich gave a preliminary talk on the parasites, and how Husserl's method could be used to combat them. Further lectures were put off until the following day, since everyone felt too disturbed and excited by their new surroundings (most of us had never been in space before) to feel like ' lessons '.

While we were on the earth side of the satellite, we could pick up television. We switched on the news at 9.30. And the first thing I saw was the face of Felix Hazard, making an impassioned speech to a vast crowd of people.

Eight hours before – at seven-thirty Berlin time – Hazard had made his first Munich speech on the glory of the Aryan race, and called for the resignation of the present social democratic government, and of the chancellor, Dr Schröder. The response had been nation-wide. Two hours later, the New Nationalist Movement announced that its leader, Ludwig Stehr, had voluntarily ceded his position to Felix Hazard. Stehr was quoted as saying that Hazard would revive the old glory of the Aryan races and lead the nation to victory. There was much talk about the ' insolent threats of racially inferior groups ', and long quotations from Gobineau,

Houston Stewart Chamberlain and Rosenberg's *Myth of the Twentieth Century.*

It was obvious what had happened. The parasites had done their work in Africa, and fixed habit patterns of revolt. Now they had turned their attention to Europe. So far, the world had taken Gwambe's revolt fairly quietly. Militant negro nationalism had become so much a matter of course in the twentieth century that no one found it too alarming; besides, most countries had defence systems that were impregnable even to hydrogen rockets. The parasites now set out to produce stronger reactions – a revival of Aryan racism. It is said that it takes two to make a quarrel; the parasites were making sure that this quarrel would not remain one-sided.

This was the biggest danger yet. Europe was in no real danger from Africa. But Africa's defence system was crude compared with that of Europe or America. It had been the African policy to spend most of its money on raising the standard of living to the European level, and the present defence system was largely the result of the generosity of Russia and China. Half a dozen well-placed hydrogen bombs could wipe out millions of Africans. In all probability, Russia and China would feel obliged to intervene, and the result was bound to be world war.

I must admit that my spirits sank lower than at any time in the past months. Our task now seemed hopeless. At this rate, the world could be at war within a week – before we returned to earth. It looked as if there was nothing we could do. It was not even certain that there would be an earth for us to return to. The next thing that would happen was easy to predict: the parasites would turn their attention to disabling each country's defence system by taking over key brains. America and Europe would cease to be impregnable as traitors sabotaged their early warning systems.

I slept for only a few hours, and got up at four to watch the nine a.m. news from London. (Our clocks, of course, were set to American time.) It was bad. The German chancellor had been assassinated, and Hazard had declared that the social democratic government was outlawed. As a true representative of the will of the German people, he appointed himself Chancellor. His party would take over the government of Germany. Their new headquarters would be the Reichstag in Berlin instead of the palace in Bonn. All members of the public were authorized to shoot members of the ' renegade government' on sight. (This later proved to be unnecessary; the social democrats accepted their dismissal, and declared their support for Hazard.) Hazard now announced his new scheme for white supremacy. When the ' inferior races' of the world had been subdued, they would be deported *en masse* to Venus – that is, about a billion negroes! This idea apparently aroused immense enthusiasm in countries all over the world, including Britain and America. (No one pointed out that even if Venus could be made habitable, the cost of shipping a billion people thirty million miles would take more money than there was in the whole world.)

We were due to pass the halfway mark to the moon at seven o'clock that evening. By this time, we would have lost television contact with the earth, although we would still be receiving radio signals. The question now arose: should we turn the nose of the ship, and stay within a day's journey of the earth? If there was going to be world war we would be better off on earth, actively combating the parasites. At least we could help to prevent the parasites from penetrating the defence system of America. It would only take one of us placed in every defence unit in America to keep the parasites at bay – and one of us in the Pentagon to make sure there was no treachery from higher up.

This seemed so obviously the best policy that we were all surprised when Holcroft opposed it. He could give no coherent reasons for opposing it; he simply said that he had a ' hunch'. Since his ' hunch' had already saved our lives once, we were inclined to pay attention to what he said. I talked to him later, and tried to get him to explore the source of his hunch. After some groping, he finally said that he felt that the further we got from earth, the better. I must admit that I was disappointed. However, our decision had been made. We went on towards the moon.

For the most part, the ten ' old hands ' among us succeeded in forgetting the threat that hung over us, and concentrated on our phenomenological problems. It was less easy to make the others forget. Many of them had left families behind them and they were naturally worried. With a great deal of bullying, we managed to make them work ten hours a day on mind discipline. It was not easy, but after the second day we began to win this particular battle. The sheer tension involved worked in our favour once we had persuaded them to forget the worries they had left on earth. It kept their efforts highly disciplined. We had none of the trouble that we'd had earlier with Merril, Philips, Leaf and Ebner.

And yet I was still dissatisfied. After fifty hours of flight, we were within forty thousand miles of the moon. And I actually had a sense that the parasites were closer than ever.

I talked about it with Reich, Flieshman and the Graus after we'd finished our classes. There were certain basic facts about the parasites that we had never got clear. Theoretically, it should make no difference whether we were in outer space or on earth. They were in the mind, so one could not get further away from them. Anyway, they had not bothered us directly since the night when they destroyed most of us. They had realized that we could be defeated indirectly through a world war.

And yet in a sense, the parasites *were* in space, for I had found them in my Percy Street rooms keeping a watch on Karel Weissman's records. How did I explain this paradox? Well, they were both in space and out of it. After all, our minds are both in space and out of it. You cannot localize

167

the mind; it does not occupy space. Yet it moves in space with our bodies.

Again, I had the feeling of some clue that was missing. We sat there, going over the whole thing slowly, step by step. I said:

'The parasites *are* in space, in a sense, because they are on earth. They came to earth deliberately to feed on the human race. Now we know that human beings all appear to have separate minds, because when each of us descends into his own mind, he loses direct contact with the others. And yet we also know that, in some deeper sense, human beings share a common mind, a kind of racial mind. We are like all the taps in a city, each one separate, and yet each drawing our water from some main reservoir . . .'

Reich interrupted (I am quoting literally from a tape recording we made):

'But you said that you defeated them by drawing on some immense deep source of energy. Would that be the original reservoir itself?'

'I suppose so,' I said.

'But, in that case, these things are living *in* the reservoir, and the energy would also be available to them. How do you account for that?'

Yes, that was it! We were getting closer. Obviously, the depth of the mind – where they lived – and the reservoir of vital energy that I had drawn upon, were two quite different things. That reservoir might be *in* the depths of the mind, but it wasn't the same thing as the depths of the mind.

'Very well,' Fleishman said, 'Where does that get us?'

It was Heinrich Grau who said slowly:

'I think I can see where it gets us. We are talking about some immense, primeval source of energy – what Bernard Shaw called the Life Force. It is the raw vitality that drives us all.'

His brother Louis interrupted with excitement:

'But why should the parasites bother with individual

168

human beings if they could steal their energy direct from the source? So obviously . . .'

'Obviously they can't,' Heinrich said. 'They have to get between the source and the human individual.'

We were not following them. I asked:

'Which means . . . ?'

'Which means that this basic source isn't available to them – is probably actively hostile to them. In other words, if we could somehow get down to this source, we'd probably have enough energy to destroy the parasites.'

I explained that this thought had been in my mind earlier, although I hadn't analysed its implications so clearly. The trouble was that I couldn't get down to the source. Every time I tried, I had a sense of inadequate will-power.

Reich said: 'But if the parasites are between you and the source, they're probably obstructing you somehow.'

We now began to see that this was a real possibility. The parasites had always used this 'obstructing' method against the human race – deliberately distracting the mind when it began to get to grips with its own secrets. We had learned how to prevent this: by penetrating to those depths of the mind from which the parasites normally operated. They had retreated to depths where we could not follow, and were probably using the same old methods against us.

So far, I had been assuming that some 'natural' cause prevented me from penetrating below a certain depth in my mind. A diver can only reach a certain depth in the sea – at which the weight of water he displaces is equal to the weight of his own body. If he wants to go deeper, he has to put heavier weights on his diving suit. But I did not know of any method of making my mind heavier so that I could descend deeper into myself, and I had been assuming that this explained my failure to penetrate deeper. But did it? Now I thought about it, I realized that what prevented me from going deeper was *a drain on my sense of purpose*. My mind seemed to go blank; my sense of individuality became more precarious. In other words, it was very possible that I was being obstructed.

I decided to test this again, and the others did the same. I closed my eyes, and made the usual descent through the memory layers. But now I found that it was difficult to pass through them. Everything seemed turbulent and violent, like swimming under the sea after a depth charge has exploded. I recollected that my dreams on the previous night had had this same violent, disturbed quality.

Why? There seemed to be no parasites around. What was causing the disturbance?

I tried hard to go lower, and succeeded, with immense difficulty, in sinking to the nursery level. But here it was worse. These wild, innocent energies had gained a kind of nervous force. They are usually characterized by a deep-breathing serenity and order, like the gentle heaving of a calm sea. Now the sea was distinctly choppy.

I knew this was as far as I could go, so I allowed myself to surface quickly. Reich was already back. His experience, of course, had been identical with my own. As we waited for the others to return, we discussed the problem. Were we, perhaps, experiencing some great psychic disturbance that affected the whole human race? Or . . .

With a sense of helpless frustration, I crossed to the port, and looked down on the great, glowing surface of the moon that spread below us. It was now a mere eight hours away. I glanced at the controls, to verify that they were compensating for the gravitation pull of the satellite. And as I did so, the fantastic idea flashed into my mind. Gravity . . . the moon. I turned to Reich, and said:

' This is probably just a stupid guess, but . . . could they be using the moon as some kind of base?'

' A base?' he said blankly. ' How could they? There aren't any people there. And they don't inhabit empty space, as far as we know.'

I shrugged. ' It's just an idea . . . to explain why our minds seem so disturbed.'

Holcroft came in at this moment, and I told him briefly what we had discovered. He closed his eyes, sat on a bed, and quickly verified that the subliminal layers of the mind were in an unusual state of disturbance. And although he had not heard my question, he turned and pointed through the front port at the moon.

' It's that. It's somehow affecting us as it affects the tides.'

I asked him: ' How do you know?'

He shrugged. ' I can tell. I can feel its pull.'

This was possible. Lunatics . . . men whose minds are affected by the gravitational pull of the moon. But why? Why should the moon affect the mind?

I asked Holcroft: ' Do you think there are parasites there?'

He shook his head.

' I don't see how there can be. And yet . . . it's somehow connected with them.'

We decided that the others had better be brought into this discussion. It was the kind of problem where anyone's ideas might shed light. So I asked them all to come in. Then I explained it as briefly as I could.

It was a nuclear physicist called Berger who came up with the only useful suggestion.

' Do you know the work of the philosopher Gurdjieff? He always said that human beings were food for the moon. He compared the human race to a flock of sheep that are being fattened for the moon . . .'

I asked Holcroft:

' Does that make sense to you?'

He said seriously:

' I think it does. There can be no doubt whatever that the moon exerts a curious pull on the human mind. This is nothing to do with gravity. We also believe that the moon was never a part of the earth or the sun – that it came from somewhere else. Perhaps it was a comet that the earth captured.

171

Its chemical composition is quite unlike the earth's. Now supposing that the moon *does* steal human energy . . . or affect it in some way.'

Reich said: 'You mean that it might be the base of the parasites?'

'No, I don't think it is. But I believe that the parasites might make some kind of use of the moon all the same. I feel it's emitting some kind of disturbing energy-psychic energy. It's a kind of giant transmitter, and the earth's a giant receiver . . .'

The others now began contributing fragments of moon legends that I had never heard. They told me about the Hörbiger cult, to which Hitler had belonged, with its belief that the earth captures a new moon every ten thousand years or so. According to Hörbiger, the present moon is earth's seventh. The other six all ended by falling on the earth and causing tremendous cataclysms that destroyed most of mankind. The flood recorded in the Bible was due to the fall of the sixth moon.

Others in the group mentioned other moon theories – Velikovsky's, Bellamy's, Saurat's – which seem to indicate that this notion of the moon as a hostile force had preoccupied many different minds.

Most of these theories sounded too absurd to take seriously. The fact remained that I was conscious that the moon was producing a definite disturbance in the pre-conscious levels of my mind. Reich also pointed out that the parasites seemed to have most power during the night. I had always assumed that this was because the mind is tired at the end of the day. Yet when I had occasionally slept during the day, and stayed awake all night, I had been dimly aware of an increased feeling of vulnerability during the night.

I asked Holcroft:

'Do you think it possible that the parasites somehow *use* this curious energy emitted by the moon – use it to interfere with human thought processes?'

But Holcroft knew as little about this as the rest of us.

Still, one thing was very clear. We had to find out whether we could get beyond the range of this disturbing influence. If, as Holcroft suggested, the moon was a gigantic transmitter and the earth a receiver, then we had to get right out of range of them both. That meant that our present course had to be changed, for it would take us in a huge arc within ten thousand miles of the moon.

I radioed Colonel Massey back in Annapolis, and explained that we wanted to change our route, and go on into outer space, aiming roughly between the present positions of Jupiter and Saturn. Massey said that he saw no reason why not: we had fuel for another fortnight. This meant that we could risk going on for another three quarters of a million miles before turning back. If he'd known earlier, he said, we could have carried enough fuel to take us halfway to Mars. I said that I thought half a million miles should be far enough from earth. That is more than twice the distance between earth and the moon.

Following Massey's instructions, I made the necessary changes in the robot control. Then I rejoined the others for supper. It was a curiously cheerful meal – considering our situation. We were hurtling beyond the moon, and penetrating regions of space where no human being had ever ventured – except the crew of the ill-fated *Proclis*. Somehow, anxieties about the earth dropped away from us, as business worries vanish on the first day of a holiday.

That night, I slept more deeply and peacefully than for several weeks.

I woke up and looked at my watch; it was half past seven. I tried to remember why I was feeling so happy. Had I had a pleasant dream, perhaps? I could recollect no dreams. I got up and walked to the rear port. The moon was an immense crescent, with its mountains clearly visible. Nearly a quarter of a million miles behind it lay the great blue-green crescent of the earth, like an immense sun. The sun itself was a blinding white, as if about to explode, and the stars all looked many times larger than on earth. The sense of delight in me rose to such a pitch of intensity that I had deliberately to suppress it.

I closed my eyes, and sank into my mind. It was calmer than yesterday, although the turbulence was still present. And now it seemed obvious to me that this turbulence was due to the moon. But its power had weakened. The result was a delightful feeling of inner calm and freedom, as if one were convalescing from an illness.

I went and woke up Reich and Holcroft. I noticed that they looked healthier and happier than I had seen them for many weeks. They were experiencing the same freedom. None of us said much, but we all felt the same enormous hope.

Nothing happened that day. We merely sat around, watching the moon recede, and observing in ourselves the steady growth of freedom. In a sense, it was the most eventful day of my life, and yet there is almost nothing I can say about it.

And it is at this point that the language problem arises. Words begin to fail because our normal language has never had to describe these experiences. I can only try to suggest a parallel. Imagine a country of tiny dwarfs, who have various words and phrases for size: large, big, enormous, immense, vast, and so on, and who, when they wish to describe the idea of immensity, say: 'As vast as a man.' What would then happen if one of the dwarfs was snatched up by an eagle, and carried into the air above Mount Everest? How could he ever find a word to explain that the mountain was so large that even a man is tiny in comparison?

This is my problem. I shall not try to take refuge in cant phrases about the impossibility of describing it in words. Nothing is indescribable in words if you take the time and the trouble. If your present language framework is inadequate, then you must carefully create a larger one.

174

Still, this is impracticable at the moment. An adequate description of what happened in the next ten days would require a long book, full of analogies. I must try to do my best with the inadequate linguistic resources available to me.

What was happening, then, was that we were moving beyond the range of the mind parasites. We understood this on the first day.

They were still present in my mind. I could tell as soon as I closed my eyes and sank into myself. I was now aware of them in the regions below the nursery. They were still beyond my reach, but I could sense their panic. They didn't like being half a million miles away from earth. As the gap widened, their panic increased. I knew then that they were creatures of low intelligence. If they had been able to think logically, they would have realized that we would be back on earth within a fortnight. They would have no difficulty surviving during this time. But they felt a wholly irrational panic, the kind of thing a child feels on leaving home. They had been on earth for a long time, swimming in the dense seas of human vitality, moving freely from one human being to another, always with a wide choice of prey. Now they felt their psychic links with the earth stretching and growing weaker, and they were frightened.

Some of us were less happy about this. We mistook the fear of the parasites for our own – which was natural, since we felt it rising from instinctive depths of our own minds. The more experienced ones among us had to maintain a constant vigil to make sure that none of our new recruits succumbed to panic. We now understood the nature of the ' space fever ' that had so far frustrated all man's efforts to penetrate far into space.

But as the days passed, we knew that we had defeated the parasites; that it would only be a matter of time before they surrendered to the panic. Every day added 120,000 miles to the distance between us and the earth. It was simply a question of how far we would have to go before they cracked.

I now found that I could descend into my mind with extraordinary ease. I could do it without effort, without even closing my eyes. At last I was beginning to understand what Teilhard de Chardin meant when he said that man's true home is the mind. I was able to move around in my mind as simply and as freely as a man with a motor car can move around the country. I could also pass through the ' nursery ' region, and float down into the ' nothingness '. But now I was aware that it was far from being a ' nothingness '. It certainly had some of the attributes of empty space – stillness, lack of all tension. But it was like the stillness at the bottom of the Pacific Ocean, where the pressure is so enormous that no creatures can live. The ' nothingness ' was pure life energy – although words are now becoming so inaccurate that they are almost meaningless.

I sometimes spent many hours in this sea of darkness, doing nothing, merely hovering. This is hard to grasp, because we are so accustomed to movement, and the parasites have so confused our habitual thought-processes. But stillness is natural to man : stillness and utter calm. Every poet knows this, for in stillness he begins to understand the greatness of his own inner powers – or ' soul ', as Wordsworth would have said. If you throw a pebble into a stormy sea, it has no effect. If you throw it into a still pond, you can see every ripple, and hear them lapping against the bank. The parasites have always kept man's mind stormy, by harnessing the disturbing energies of the moon, and this is why man has never been able to make use of his enormous powers. Poets and so-called ' men of genius ' are the only ones who even suspect the existence of such powers.

A point came where we had a decision to take. We had been out from earth for ten days. We had enough fuel to take us back as far as the nearest artificial satellite. The mind parasites were obviously near breaking point. Could we risk pushing on into space, and perhaps finding ourselves stranded? We had ceased to use all electrical equipment, knowing that the energy would be needed. The ship had immense photon sails which had been spread as soon as we were out of the earth's atmosphere, and to some extent we were pushed onward by the pressure of sunlight. Much of the energy used to drive the ship's engines also came from the sun. But, obviously, the photon sails would be of no use for returning to earth, for ' tacking' with a space ship is infinitely more complicated than with a yacht. It was true that we used very little energy as we went onward; we were ' free-wheeling' into space, the only opposing forces being the gravitational pull of distant planets, and of the meteorites that swooped past us at a rate of two or three an hour.

We decided to risk it. Somehow, it was impossible to feel pessimistic about our prospects of returning to earth. And so we went on steadily, ignoring the problems, waiting for the parasites to loosen their grip.

It happened on the fourteenth day, and none of us anticipated what it would be like. During the morning, I was aware of their increasing fear and of their hatred. My mind became cloudier and more turbulent than at any time since we left the moon. I was sitting with Reich near the rear port, staring back towards the earth. Suddenly his face distorted with fear, and I felt a wave of panic. I looked out of the port to see if he had seen something that frightened him. When I looked back, his face had become grey, and he looked like a very sick man. And then he shuddered, closed his eyes for a moment – and became transformed. He began to roar with laughter, but it was the healthy laughter of enormous delight. And at that moment, I felt an awful tearing feeling in the depths of my being, a pain as if some living creature were trying to eat its way out of me. Physical and mental agony became identical. It seemed obvious that I could not survive. Then I heard Reich yelling in my ear: ' It's all right! We've *beaten* them. They're leaving!' Now the thing became atrocious. Something infinitely evil and slimy was pushing its way from inside me. For a moment, I realized that I had been wrong to think of the parasites as separate beings. They were one; they were ' It ', something I can only compare to an immense, jelly-like octopus whose tentacles are separated from its body and can move about like individuals. It was incredibly nasty, like feeling a pain under your clothes, and finding that some great carnivorous slug has eaten its way halfway into your body. Now this infinitely vile thing was coming out of its lair, and I could feel its hatred of me, a hatred so powerful and maniacal that it almost needs a new word.

Then – the infinite, inexpressible relief of knowing it was gone. My reaction was unlike Reich's. The happiness and gratitude that rose in me were so strong that I felt as if my heart would burst, and tears blinded my eyes so that the sun's light became a great glare that reminded me of swimming under water when I was a child. When this passed away, I felt like a convalescent who has just seen the doctors removing some loathsome cancer from inside him.

The others were eating in the next room. We rushed in and told them what had happened. Everyone became immensely excited and began asking us questions. No one else had started to feel the preliminary pains. I presume that it was our position – looking back towards the earth – that had caused us to experience it first. So we advised the others to move into the other room – and warned them what to expect. Then Reich and I went to the other end of the ship, where everything was in darkness, to make our first trip into the new free country of the mind.

And this is the point where I become aware that anything I say will be a lie. So I must make an effort to explain, rather than try to make everyday language do a job for which it was never intended.

Freedom is the most important experience that can happen to human beings. In ordinary life, we experience it moment·

arily when some emergency calls upon all our energies, and then is suddenly overcome. What happens then is that the mind becomes an eagle, no longer tied to the immediate present.

The greatest human problem is that we are all tied to the present. This is because we are machines, and our free will is almost infinitesimal. Our body is an elaborate machine, just like a motor car. Or perhaps a better simile would be those 'powered' artificial limbs worn by people who have lost an arm or leg. These limbs, with their almost indestructible power units, are as responsive as our real arms and legs, and I am told that a man who has worn them for years can totally forget that they are not real limbs. But if the power unit should break down, he quickly realizes that his limb is only a machine, and that his own will-power plays a very small part in its movements.

Well, this is true of all of us. We have far less will-power than we believe. This means that we have almost no real freedom. This hardly matters most of the time, because the 'machine' – our bodies and brains – is doing what we want anyway: eating and drinking and excreting and sleeping and making love and the rest.

But poets and mystics have moments of freedom when they suddenly realize that they want the 'machine' to do something far more interesting. They want the mind to be able to detach itself from the world at a moment's notice, and float above it. Our attention is usually fixed upon minute particulars, actual objects around us, like a car in gear. Then, in certain moments, the car goes into 'neutral'; the mind ceases to be engaged with trivial particulars, and finds itself free. Instead of being tied to the dull reality of the present, it is free to choose which reality it prefers to contemplate. When your mind is 'in gear', you can use your memory to recall yesterday, or to create a picture of a place on the other side of the world. But the picture remains dim, like a candle in the sunlight, or a mere ghost. In the 'poetic' moments,

179

the moments of freedom, *yesterday becomes as real as now*.

If we could learn the trick of putting the mind in and out of gear, man would have the secret of godhead. But no trick is more difficult to learn. We are ruled by habit. Our bodies are robots that insist on doing what they have been doing for the past million years: eating, drinking, excreting, making love – and attending to the present.

Now my first discovery of the existence of the parasites enabled me to break the ' habit ', which the parasites had been carefully fostering and strengthening. What it meant was that I suddenly realized that it is not in the nature of things that man should get brief glimpses of freedom, his ' intimations of immortality ', and then lose them immediately. There is no reason why he should not experience them for ten hours a day if he likes. (More than that would be harmful, because after all, we have to attend to the trivialities of the moment *sometime*.)

Since the beginning of August – when I first read Karel's *Historical Reflections* – I had been continually awake to the possibilities of my own freedom, and this in itself meant that I had broken the chain that binds most human beings. The parasites relied mainly on habit and ignorance to keep the human race in chains. But they had also established themselves at a deep level of the human psyche, where they could ' drink ' the energies that human beings draw from their wellspring of vitality.

I should try to make this point quite clear. If man had not been an ' evolutionary animal ', the parasites would have found a permanent host. There would never have been the faintest chance of man discovering their existence. They could have spent eternity happily ' tapping ' man's power cable, and man would never have been any the wiser. But a small percentage of the human race – about a twentieth, to be precise – are evolutionary animals with a deep and powerful urge to become truly free. These men had to be ' distracted ', and for this reason, the parasites had to move towards the surface of the mind, to manipulate their puppets. This was how they had given themselves away.

I have said that man draws his power from a secret life source in the depths of his being. This source is man's inviolable centre of gravity, his real being. It is completely indestructible. The parasites therefore had no access to it. All they could do was to ' steal ' energy in transit from this deep source to man's conscious being.

And now I can perhaps explain something of what I discovered when I made a fresh attempt to enter into myself, although my warning about language must be constantly borne in mind.

First of all, I observed an extraordinary stillness in my mind. There was no longer any turbulence of any kind. This was because it was at last *my* mind, with no interlopers. At last, it was my own kingdom.

This also made an immense difference to my dreams and memories. Anyone who has tried to sleep when his brain is over-tired, or he has a touch of fever, knows that awful sensation when all the thoughts seem to be fishes rushing about at a great speed, and they all seem *alien*. The inside of the head, which should be a ' fine and private place ', is like a fairground crowded with strangers. Well, I had never realized until this moment how far the brain is always a fairground crowded with parasites. For now it was completely calm and silent. My memories stood in orderly arrays, like troops at a royal salute. At a single order, I could make any one of them step forward. I realized the truth of the statement that everything that has happened to us is carefully stored in the memory. Memories of my earliest childhood were as accessible as memories of yesterday. What is more, memories of previous lives were now connected in a continuous sequence with memories of my present life. My mind was like a completely calm sea, that reflects the sky like a mirror, and whose water is so clear that the bottom is as visible as the surface. I understand what Jacob Boehme meant when he talked of a ' sabbath of the spirit '. For the very first time in my life, I was in contact with *reality*. No more fever, no more nightmare, no more delusions. The thing that astounded me most was the tremendous strength of human beings, to have succeeded in living, in spite of the terrible veil of insanity that hides them from reality. They must be one of the hardiest species in the universe.

Now I descended through my mind like a man walking through the halls of a castle. For the first time, I knew what I was. I knew that this *was me*. It was not ' my mind ', because the adjective ' my ' refers to only a minute section of my being. It was all me.

I penetrated through the ' nursery ' layers, those bright energies whose purpose is to establish man's moral balance, to act as moral policemen. When a man is tempted to believe the world is evil, and has to be fought with evil, these powers are drawn to the surface as white blood corpuscles are drawn to an infected area of the body. All this was clear to me for the first time.

Below them was the great sea of motionless life. It was now no longer a sea of darkness and nothingness. As I descended into it, I became aware that it had a quality of luminescence and warmth. This time, there was no obstacle, no force of blindness and malevolence to push me back.

And then I began to understand something which is almost impossible to express. There was no point in going deeper. Those depths contained pure life, and yet, in a sense, they also contained death, the death of the body and of consciousness. The thing we call ' life ' on earth is a combination of the pure life forces with the body; it is liaison between life and the inanimate. I say ' the inanimate ' because ' matter ' would be the wrong word. All matter is alive in so far as it exists. The key word here is ' existence '. No human being can understand the word ' existence ' because he is *in* it. But to

182

exist is not a passive quality; it is to *thrust out* from non-existence. Existence in itself is a shout of affirmation. To exist is to defy non-existence.

You can see that it is all a problem of language. I am being forced to make do with one or two words when I need about fifty. It is not quite analogous to describing colours to a blind man, because no human being is entirely ' blind '; we all have glimpses of freedom. But freedom has as many colours as the spectrum.*

All this means that in trying to descend towards the ' source ' of my life I was leaving behind the realm of existence, for the source does not exist; that is to say, it does not stand out from non-existence.

All this was freedom; the beautiful, inexpressible intoxication of freedom. My mind was my own; and I was the first human being to achieve superhumanity. And yet I had to leave these fascinating prospects to consider the problem that had brought us into outer space: the earth and the mind parasites. So I came reluctantly back to the surface. And I looked on Reich as a stranger, and saw that he was looking at me in the same way. We smiled at one another, like two actors who have just finished rehearsing a scene in which they are enemies. I said: ' What happens now?'

He said: ' How far did you get?'

' Not far. There was no point.'

' What powers can we draw upon?'

' I'm still not sure. I'd like the advice of the others.'

We went back into the other room. Fifteen of them had lost their parasites, and were helping the others. Some of the new recruits were in such agony that they were likely to damage themselves, like a mother who writhes around the floor as she gives birth. It cost us a considerable effort to

* The above passage comes from a manuscript written in 2005. (M.F.-WHA-3271). We have included it for the sake of continuity. This whole problem is covered in minute detail in Austin's monumental *Life, Being and Language* (2025 - 2041), particularly Vol. 8, chaps 7 - 9.

soothe them, since force would have been of no use – it would only have intensified their terror. One man kept screaming: 'Turn the ship, turn the ship, it's killing me.' The creature inside him was obviously trying to force him to make us return to earth. His release came twenty minutes later, and he was so exhausted that he immediately fell asleep.

By eight o'clock that evening, it was all over. Most of the new recruits were so dazed that they could hardly speak. They were suffering from an extreme version of the ' double exposure ' effect. They knew they were not themselves – not the people they had always taken themselves for – but they had not yet discovered that these strange depths of alien being *were* themselves. There was no point in trying to explain, since this would confine them to the conscious part of the personality; they had to find out for themselves.

At all events, about ten of us were perfectly clear headed. We now realized that there could be no problem about fuel for the rocket. Our united PK powers could drive this rocket as far as Pluto at a thousand times its present speed. But that would serve no purpose. We had to go back to earth, and to decide how we intended to fight the parasites. It would not be difficult to destroy Gwambe and Hazard, but this would only be a temporary expedient. The parasites could create new Gwambes and Hazards at will. And we could not destroy all their followers, or undertake to ' re-programme ' their minds. We had to play this game according to the parasites' rules. It was like a game of chess, with human beings for pawns.

We discussed it far into the night without arriving at any definite plan. I had a feeling that we were on the wrong track altogether. We were thinking in terms of out-generalling the parasites. But there must be some other way . . .

At three o'clock in the morning, Reich woke me up. I should say that his mind woke me up, for he was in the next room. We lay in the dark, and conversed telepathically. He had not been to sleep; instead, he had been thinking back, slowly and methodically, over the whole problem.

He said:

'I've been trying to correlate everything we know about these creatures. Because there's one thing that baffles me. Why should they hate leaving the earth so much? If they're in the mind, it should not make any difference to them where they are.'

I suggested: 'Because they exist at a level of the mind that's common to all human beings – Jung's racial unconscious.'

'That's still no answer. Distance makes no difference to thought. I can communicate telepathically with someone on earth as easily as with you. So we're still a part of the human subconscious mind. In that case, they ought to be as comfortable here as back on earth.'

I asked: 'What do you think?'

'I still think it has something to do with the moon.'

'You think they use it as a base?'

'No. It's something far more complicated than that. Listen to me, and tell me if this makes sense to you. Let's start with the Kadath business. We know that all that stuff about the 'Great Old Ones' was untrue. We assume therefore that there is no real connection between the mind parasites and Kadath – that they simply used it as a gigantic red herring to keep man looking for his enemies *outside* himself. Now this is probably true. But even so, doesn't Kadath offer us certain clues? The first thing it proves beyond all shadow of doubt is that the usual dating of human history is a mistake. According to geology, man is about a million years old. All that means is that we haven't found any human remains that date back further than that.'

'And the earliest remains indicate that he hadn't progressed far beyond the ape a million years ago,' I reminded him.

'Who hadn't? Pekin Man? Australopithecus? How do

we know they were the *only* kind of man? Don't forget that the Romans had a high degree of civilization when the British were still savages. And the Hittites were civilized when the Romans and Greeks were still savages. It's all relative. Civilization tends to develop in pockets. Well, the one thing we know about the evolutionary process is that it favours intelligence. So why should we make the curious assumption that man only appeared a million years ago? We know that dinosaurs and mammoths and giant sloths – and even horses – existed millions of years before that. Man must have had some kind of primitive, ape-like ancestor back in the Jurassic. He didn't just appear from nowhere.

' You'll agree that the existence of Kadath bears out this theory? The only alternative theory is that the inhabitants of Kadath came from another planet.

' So we concede that man is a great deal older than a million years. But that raises the problem of why civilization didn't develop sooner. And there again, I'm inclined to pay attention to the various myths about the destruction of the world – the great flood, and so on. Now, supposing the various moon-cranks are right, and there *is* some truth in the notion that the great flood was caused by the moon falling on the earth?'

I was not entirely with him so far. I could not see what these speculations had to do with the mind parasites.

' You will in a moment. If we correlate the various flood myths, we arrive at the conclusion that the flood took place in fairly recent human history – say around five thousand B.C. Supposing, then, the flood *was* caused by the moon circling closer to the earth, as Hörbiger suggests? Could this mean that our present moon has been circling the earth for only about seven thousand years?'

' I agree it's possible.'*

* ' A curious line of maritime deposits can be traced from Lake Umayo, in the Peruvian Andes, (13,000 feet above sea level) extending for three hundred and seventy-five miles southward to Lake Coipusa.

'But as an archaeologist, would you say there is any real evidence to support the idea – or is it just wild guesswork?'

'I think there's a great deal of evidence – I said as much in a book I wrote twenty years ago. But I still can't see any connection with the parasites.'

'I'll tell you. I've been brooding on this question of the origin of the parasites. Weissman said he thought they landed on earth about two hundred years ago. But we know they don't like outer space. So where did they come from?'

'The moon?'

'Possibly. But that's still supposing that they can exist apart from the human mind.'

And, suddenly, I saw what he meant. Of course! We now had an important clue about the origin of the parasites – they didn't like existing apart from the mass of mankind. Why shouldn't they?

The answer was so shatteringly simple that it was unbelievable. They couldn't exist apart from mankind *because they were mankind*. The clue was there in the first sentence of Weissman's *Historical Reflections*: 'It has been my conviction . . . that the human race is being attacked by a sort

The line is curved, ending some eight hundred feet below its beginning, which is close to the equator. The disciples of Hörbiger and Bellamy argue – convincingly, in my opinion – that these strange deposits indicate that the sea once formed a kind of bulge around the equator. This could only have been due to the moon being far closer to the earth than at present, and circling at a far greater speed, so that the " tide " never had time to retreat. The ruins of Tiahuanaco, near Lake Titicaca, add another curious fragment to this puzzle. It could be said to be " above the Pacific Ocean " – twelve thousand feet above it; yet there are many indications that it was a port more than ten thousand years ago. The ruins are of such size that one can only surmise that they were built by giants – that is to say, by men who could grow to two or three times the present average height by reason of the lesser gravitational pull of the earth (which the moon would neutralize) . . . Stranger still is the fact that among these ruined cities of the Andes the bones of toxodons have been unearthed – and the toxodon is an animal that vanished from the earth a million years ago. Heads of toxodons are carved on some of the ruins of Tiahuanaco '. G. Austin, *Frontiers of Archaeology*, P. 87. London 1983.

of mind cancer'. A cancer. And a cancer cannot live apart from the body of its host.

But what causes a physical cancer? This was one of the problems whose answer is self-evident to anyone who has explored his own mind. It springs from the same root as the 'split personality'. Man is a continent, but his conscious mind is no larger than a back-garden. This means that man consists almost entirely of *unrealized potentialities*. The so-called 'great men' are the men who have had the courage to realize some of these potentialities. The 'average man' is too timid and cowardly to make the attempt. He prefers the security of the back-garden.

Now a 'split personality' occurs when some of these un-realized potentialities take their revenge. So, for example, a timid man, who possesses a strong sexual urge which he tries to suppress, wakes up one day to find that he has committed a sexual assault. He tries to excuse himself by saying that it was as if 'another being' took over his body and committed the assault. But that 'other being' was really himself – a part of himself that he was too cowardly to recognize.

Cancer is also caused by the 'unrealized potentialities' taking their revenge. The earliest cancer research workers noticed that it is a disease of frustration or of old age. Men who have the courage to fulfil themselves do not die of can-cer. But men who possess potentialities, but lack the courage to express them, form a high proportion of cancer patients. Their life-mistrust poisons their souls.

Both cancer and split personality become impossible as soon as a man learns to descend into his inner-being, for it becomes impossible for these pockets of frustration to build up.

In a sense, Karel Weissman was right: the 'parasites' *did* appear about two centuries ago. The men of previous cen-turies were so preoccupied with holding body and soul to-gether that they had no time to be frustrated. They were more 'unified' than modern man; they lived on a more instinctive level. Then man reached a watershed in his evolution, a point where he had to become a more conscious, more intellectual and self-critical being. The gap between his conscious level and his instinctive level grew wider. And suddenly, cancer and schizophrenia ceased to be rare diseases and became commonplace. But what was the significance of the moon in all this?

Again, cancer provides the clue. Cancer is due to a general drop in the level of vitality, due to frustration or old age. But this in itself is not sufficient to start the cancer. There has to be some *specific* irritant, a bruise, for example. If we consider life as a kind of electrical force that inhabits a human body, as magnetism inhabits a magnet, then we could say that the bruised flesh is no longer capable of carrying the same magnetic current as the rest. It slips to a lower level and proceeds to develop on its own, a kind of ' split personality '.

If oysters were higher organisms, the irritant of the pearl would be enough to cause cancer.

Reich's theory of the mind parasites was roughly this:

About ten thousand years ago, the moon was pulled slowly towards the earth by earth's gravitation. It was probably earth's third or fourth moon. It took about two thousand years before it finally crashed on the earth, splitting in pieces. The sea, which had been held near the equator by the moon's gravity, was now able to rush back over the earth in a huge tidal wave, destroying all that existed of civilization. (But not the Kadath civilization; that had been destroyed by a much earlier moon.)

For a thousand years or so, earth had no moon, and very little life. Then it captured another space-wanderer, another giant meteorite – our present moon. But it had captured an exceedingly dangerous satellite. For this new moon was ' radioactive ' with strange forces, forces that could exercise a disturbing effect on the human mind.

Any theories about the origin of these forces is guesswork.

Reich's theory – which I think as likely as any – was as follows: the moon had once been part of some larger body, perhaps a sun, and had been inhabited by creatures who were 'bodiless' in the physical sense. This is less absurd than it sounds. Scientists used to declare that certain planets could never contain life because life could not survive under their conditions; they discovered that life can gain a foothold under the most unpromising conditions. Life that could gain a foothold on the sun would certainly not be 'physical' in the sense that we understand it.

A great burning fragment had been torn from this sun by a passing comet, and the hot gases had condensed into the moon as we know it today, gradually destroying its inhabitants. But since they were not 'bodies' in the earthly sense, they could not die in the ordinary way. They tried to adapt to the cooling matter of their world, becoming a part of the molecular structure of the solid as they had once been a part of the structure of the hot gas.

So the moon remains 'radio-active' with a strange, alien life.

If the moon had not been captured by our earth, this alien life would have died long ago, for life can only exist where the second law of thermodynamics operates – that is to say, where there is energy flowing from a higher to a lower level. But the moon was kept 'alive' by the closeness of the earth, a planet seething with life and energy. Its presence was like the continual smell of a hot dinner to a starving man. And as the human race slowly gained a new foothold on the earth, men were dimly and instinctively aware of the living presence of the moon.

And here, I believe, we have the answer to the question about the origin of the parasites – of the 'irritant' that caused the cancer. Lower forms of life – fishes and mammals – are unaffected by the 'watchers'; they live on an instinctive level, and the alien presence seems quite natural to them. But man slowly proceeds to become the master of the earth, and he does this by developing his intellect, his conscious mind. So he becomes 'split', separated from his instinctive drives. Frustrations build up, and turn into fiery little pockets of suppressed energy. And at this point, the 'irritant' of the moon, the constant psychic pressure of half-frozen life, begins to produce its predictable effects. The mind-cancers begin to develop.

It may seem that all this theorizing was built upon rather slender evidence. This is not true. It was all built upon logic – starting from that puzzling question: Why were the parasites afraid of outer space?

An immediate answer suggested itself. As man loses touch with his 'inner being', his instinctive depths, he finds himself trapped in the world of consciousness, that is to say, *in the world of other people.* Any poet knows this truth; when other people sicken him, he turns to hidden resources of power inside himself, and he knows then that other people don't matter a damn. He knows that the 'secret life' inside him is the reality; other people are mere shadows in comparison. But the 'shadows' themselves cling to one another. 'Man is a political animal,' said Aristotle, telling one of the greatest lies in human history. For every man has more in common with the hills, or with the stars, than with other men.

The poet is a more or less unified being; he has not lost touch with his inner powers. But it is the other men, the 'shadows', who are subject to mind-cancer. For them, human society is the reality. They are entirely concerned with its personal little values, with its pettiness and malice and self-seeking. And since the parasites are a projection of these creatures, is it surprising that the parasites themselves cling to human society? They had no place in our space ship, for we were all men who knew the secret: that man is never 'alone', for he is directly connected to the universal power-house.

191

In other words, even if we had not gone out in space, our minds would have been no harbour for the parasites. In us, the cancer was slowly dying of starvation. Our journey into space had only hastened the process. As we separated from the rest of humankind, our first sensation was a terrible fear and loneliness, like a child being separated from its mother for the first time. In that moment, one faces the great question. Is man really a social being who has no existence apart from other men? If that is true, then all our human values are lies: goodness, truth, love, religion and the rest – for these values are, by definition, absolute, more important than other human beings.

That fear caused a new turning-inward, to the 'source of power, meaning and purpose'. Those false telephone wires that connect us to other human beings are cut. This does not mean that other human beings cease to be important. They become far more important, for you realize that, in a certain sense, they are immortal. But you become aware that all our so-called 'human' values are false, based on man's devaluation of himself.

That was why the parasites were forced to leave us. The deeper we journeyed into space, the more certainly we faced that truth: that other men do not supply our values. Other men do not matter in the sense we have always believed. Man is not alone. You could be the last man alive in the universe, and you would not be alone.

Reich and I talked for the rest of the night. And when dawn came – or the hour that would be dawn on earth – something had happened to both of us. Within the past few hours we had changed. The chrysalis had become the butterfly.

We no longer belonged to the earth. This empty space around us was our home just as much as that absurd little green globe that was two million miles behind us.

It was a little frightening. It felt like being a beggar who suddenly inherits a fortune. He looks at the rows of servants waiting for his orders; he contemplates all the things he could do with so much money; he looks at the vast estates that now belong to him . . . and his mind reels; he experiences a certain vertigo, a terror of freedom.

There was so much to be explored, so many things we didn't know . . .

But first, there was another task: to bring home this knowledge to the others.

And although the earth was no longer our home, there could be no doubt of what we had to do next. We had become policemen of the universe.

I went across to the robot control panel. A week earlier, I'd had to get detailed instructions from Colonel Massey. Now the thing seemed as simple as a child's toy. I quickly made the necessary adjustments and pressed the re-programming switch. The ship immediately retracted its photon sails, and fired a turning rocket. We began to turn in a slow, gentle arc. The others woke up and came to see what was happening.

I said: 'We're returning to earth. Give me your help in making this ship go faster.'

We locked our minds in parallel, and began to induce a delicate alternating current of will. And then, very slowly, we allowed it to discharge over the back of the ship. It was as if a giant hand had squeezed the ship like a great fish. We felt the spurt of acceleration, and did it again. Again the ship responded. We tried stronger charges; the ship vibrated but responded. This was a delicate and dangerous business. We could apply a force equal to a dozen hydrogen bombs, but it had to be applied in such a manner that it would be transformed into linear velocity. Carelessly applied, it could wreck the ship and disintegrate it into atomic dust. Reich and I could now survive this, but the others couldn't.

There was something amusing in being two million miles out in space in this absurd, crude tin rocket, that seemed to have been designed by imbeciles. Reich and I agreed that one of our first tasks on reaching the earth would be to show men how to construct a real space ship.

The easiest and quickest way to explain to the others was to communicate telepathically. For this purpose, we all held hands in a circle, as in a seance. It took only about five seconds to communicate to them what had taken us most of the night to understand. For, in a sense, it was something they already knew. We had explored the road in the dark; they were walking it by daylight.

This was in itself an interesting experience. I had not looked at Reich during the night – we had been in different rooms. Neither had I bothered to look at my own face in the mirror. But as soon as we had transmitted our knowledge to the others, we saw a remarkable change come over them. It was, of course, to be expected, and yet to see it on so many faces at once was a strange sight. The usual adjectives fail to express it. I could say that they became ' nobler ' or greater, but that is a long way from the truth. It would be more accurate to say that they became child-like. But the sense of this must be understood. If you look into the face of a very young baby – say six months old – and then into that of an old man, you suddenly understand that subtle quality known as life, joy, magic. No matter how wise and good the old man is, he lacks it. But if the child is happy and intelligent, it radiates this quality, and it is almost painful to see, because he obviously belongs to a brighter universe. He is still half-angel. Adults – even the greatest – devalue life: a baby trusts and affirms with its whole being.

It was this quality of pure life that suddenly descended into the breakfast room of the space rocket, and it is no exaggeration to say that it felt like the dawn of creation. Seeing it in one another deepened the power and certainty in each one of us.

And it was this that brought a new level of knowledge. When I had said to them: ' Man is not alone ', I had understood what I meant, but all its implications were not clear to me; I was speaking about the source of power, meaning and purpose. Now I realized that, in a far more obvious and simple sense, we were not alone. We had joined the police of the universe, and there were others. Our minds now made instant contact with these others. It was as if we had sent out a signal which had instantly been picked up by a hundred receivers, who immediately signalled their presence back to us. The nearest of these receivers was situated only about four thousand million miles away, a cruising ship from a planet in the Proxima Centauri system.

I shall say no more about this, since it plays no further part in my story.

We were travelling at a speed of about a hundred thousand miles an hour. With two million miles to cover, this meant we were about twenty hours from earth. The moon, of course, revolves about a quarter of a million miles from earth. and it was still between us and the earth – which meant that we would be passing it in about seventeen and a half hours. Our business, we knew, lay with the moon.

There was no thought, at this stage, of actually moving the moon. Its weight is approximately 5×10^{15} tons – that is to say, five thousand billion tons. As yet, we had no idea of how much mass our combined PK powers could move, but there seemed little enough chance that they were great enough for this task. Besides, what if we *did* succeed in pushing off the moon into outer space? The constant irritant upon the human psyche would vanish; but it had now done its work. The mind parasites would survive in any case.

In spite of this, it was obvious that the moon was the key. It was something that demanded immediate investigation.

We were within fifty thousand miles of the moon before we again became aware of its pull. Reich and I looked at one another. The significance of this fact was obvious. In some obscure way, the moon was ' aware ' of us. On our way out from the earth, it had been aware of us from the moment we left the earth, and its ' attention ' had continued to focus on us long after we had passed beyond it. Now we were approaching from behind, and it did not ' notice ' us until we were within a mere fifty thousand miles.

The clouding of the faculties that we had experienced on the way out was now less marked. We knew what it was: trapped life forces that somehow observed us hopefully. The ' clouding ' was actually an emotional disturbance. But once you became aware of its nature, it was not difficult to combat.

This time, we turned the space ship directly into the moon. We began to brake immediately. Half an hour later, we landed gently, throwing up a great cloud of silvery moondust.

I had been to the moon before, and it had merely seemed a dead rock. Now it was no longer dead; it was a tortured living landscape, and the sense of tragedy was enormous, like looking on the burnt-out shell of a building where you know a thousand people had died.

We wasted no time in trying the experiment that had brought us here. Without leaving the space ship (for we had no space suits, not having expected to land anywhere), we directed a beam of will-power at an immense mass of porous rock that looked like a great ant hill. Twelve of us were linked in parallel, and the power we exerted could have blasted a crater ten miles wide. The whole of the ' ant-hill ' – a mass about a mile high – disintegrated like the Abhoth block, turning into a fine dust that formed a kind of fog around the space ship. There was also considerable heat that made us all uncomfortable for ten minutes. And yet as the rock disintegrated, we all experienced for a moment a tingling of pure joy, like a very faint electric current. It was impossible to doubt. We had released the trapped life forces. But since they now had no ' body ', they vanished, dissipated in space.

196

There was something dreadfully oppressive about the moon. Shelley had exhibited a sixth sense when he asked ' Art thou pale for weariness?' And Yeats had shown almost frightening perception when he compared the moon to an idiot staggering through the sky. This was what was wrong. It was like visiting a tormented soul in bedlam.

Half an hour later, the moon lay far behind us, and the whole of the front port was occupied with the misty blue globe of the earth. This is always an exciting moment – to see the moon behind you, the earth in front of you, both about the same size. But on this occasion, we still had business with the moon.

We wished to establish how far it could be influenced by psychokinetic force. It will readily be seen that this had to be done from a position midway between the earth and the moon, since we had to ' brace' ourselves against the earth. Obviously, we could exert no force from our space ship; the moon's incomparably greater mass would turn such force against ourselves and destroy us. Our ship was merely the third angle of a flattened triangle.

This was a difficult exercise. First of all, it involved all of us for the first time – fifty minds in parallel. This actually proved to be the most difficult part of the problem. Most of them were barely aware of their powers of psychokinesis, and now they were being asked to run these immature powers in double harness with a crowd of other people. Fleishman, Reich and myself had to act as directors of the force. What we were doing was highly dangerous. Never had the space ship seemed so tinny and crude. One man losing control for a moment could easily destroy us all. So the three of us concentrated upon preventing accidents, while Holcroft and Ebner co-ordinated the attempt to build up the vibratory wave of PK energy. Then it was necessary to ' feel' our way to the earth; and this in itself produced a shock. It was suddenly like being back in Washington. Earth was transmitting ' life' as powerfully as the moon; not frustrated. imprisoned life, but fear and neurosis. The correctness of Reich's theory about the mind parasites became immediately obvious. The people of earth were building up panic waves just as we were building up psychic energy; this panic removed them further from their true selves, and created a cancerous shadow, an alter-ego, that immediately achieved a strange independent reality – as you can sometimes look at your reflection in the mirror and imagine it alive.

Once we had established our contact with earth, we were in a position to exert a double leverage on the moon – a direct beam of PK energy from the space ship, and a reflected beam from the earth.

The point of this experiment was not to affect the moon in any way, but to gauge our response to it, as a cricketer might weigh the ball in his hand. I have said that the sensation of using PK energy is not very different from the sensation of actually touching something. The only difference is that its range is far greater. In this case, once we had established the reflected beam from earth, we could actually gauge the moon's resistance. This meant simply exerting an increasing force, and finding out what happened. I had no direct experience, of course; it was all Reich, Fleishman and I could do to 'steady' the force, to prevent its vibrations from wrecking the ship. We were aware of its increased power by the increase in the vibrations. Finally, I sharply ordered them to stop. It was becoming too dangerous.

I asked Holcroft what happened. He said:

'I'm not sure, but I think we got a response. It's not difficult to encompass the moon. But it's hard to say how much pressure would affect it. We'd have to try again from earth.'

He meant, of course, that the PK beam had been able to explore the shape of the moon. But we still had no idea of whether it could be moved by PK force.

We were all exhausted. Most of us slept for the remaining hour of our journey to earth.

At nine o'clock we fired the braking jets and slowed down

to a thousand miles an hour. At 9.17, we entered earth's atmosphere, and cut off all power. Massey's control beam now picked us up, and we were able to leave the rest to him. We landed at a few minutes before ten.

It felt like coming back after a thousand years. Everything *in us* had changed so completely that the earth itself seemed a changed place. And the first thing we noticed was, perhaps, predictable. Everything seemed infinitely more beautiful than we had remembered it. This came as a shock: it was something we had not noticed on the moon, because of the satellite's disturbing influence.

On the other hand, the human beings who greeted us seemed alien and repulsive, little better than apes. It was suddenly incredible that these morons could inhabit this infinitely beautiful world and yet remain so blind and stupid. We had to remind ourselves that man's blindness is an evolutionary mechanism.

Instinctively, we all shielded ourselves from the gaze of other men, doing our best to appear unchanged. We felt the shame that a happy person feels among hopeless misery.

Massey looked very tired and ill. He said:

' Well, sir, any luck?'

' I think so,' I said.

His face changed, and the fatigue fell away. I felt a sudden wave of affection for him. These creatures might be little more than idiots, yet they were still brothers. I put my hand on his arm, and let some of the life flow out of me into him. It was a pleasure to see how quickly he became transformed – to watch the energy and optimism straightening his shoulders and taking the lines out of his face. I said:

' Tell me what's been happening since we left.'

The situation was serious. With tremendous speed and total ruthlessness, Gwambe had occupied Jordan, Syria, Turkey and Bulgaria. Where there was resistance, inhabitants had been destroyed by the thousand. A cosmic ray accumulator, that had been developed by African and European scientists for use in sub-atomic physics, had been turned into a weapon of war by the addition of a geronized-tungsten reflector, and all the inhabitants of Jerusalem had been destroyed in a few minutes. From then on, there had been no resistance. An hour before we landed, Italy had surrendered, and offered Gwambe passage through Italian territory. The German armies were massed along the frontiers of Styria and Yugoslavia, but the first major clash of the war had not taken place. The Germans were threatening to use the hydrogen bomb if Gwambe used his cosmic ray accumulator, so it seemed probable that a long drawn out 'conventional' war would now follow. Fourteen high explosive rockets had penetrated the American air defences, and one of them had started a fire that had been raging in Los Angeles for the past week. It was difficult for the Americans to counter-attack with rockets because Gwambe's armies were diffused over such an enormous area; but earlier in the day the president had announced that in future an African town would be destroyed by rockets every time an African rocket penetrated the American defence system.

But it was obvious to everyone that this was not a war that anyone could hope to win. Each retaliatory measure was only another step towards mutual destruction. The general feeling about Gwambe was that he was a homicidal maniac who constituted as great a threat to his own people as to the rest of the world.

Strangely enough, no one had yet realized that Hazard was equally insane and dangerous. During the fortnight when Gwambe was occupying the Mediterranean countries, Germany and Austria were mobilizing. Cape Town, Bulawayo and Livingstone had been heavily damaged by German rockets, but so far there had been no *concerted* act of war against Africa. But when it had been rumoured that Hazard was moving mobile launching sites for hydrogen rockets into Austria, both the Russian Premier and the American President had appealed to him not to use atomic weapons.

Hazard's reply had been noncommittal. It seemed to be generally felt that he would behave sensibly. We knew better. So did President Melville, but he had had the sense to keep this to himself.

A rocket plane took us to Washington; before midnight, we were eating a meal with the President. He also looked exhausted and ill, but half an hour with us restored his spirits. The White House domestic staff did an admirable job of providing a scratch meal for the fifty of us in the great dining-room. Almost the first thing he said to me was:

' I don't know how you can look so unconcerned.'

' Because I think we can stop this war.'

I knew that this was what he wanted to hear. I did not add that it suddenly seemed unimportant to me whether or not the human race destroyed itself. It was irritating to be back among these squalid, quarrelsome, small-minded humans.

He asked how we proposed to stop the war.

' First of all, President, we want you to get on to the central television agency and announce that you will be appearing in six hours' time to make an announcement that concerns the whole world.'

' And can you tell me what it is?'

' I'm not yet sure. But I think it will concern the moon.'

At a quarter past midnight, we were all out on the White House lawn. Clouds obscured the sky, and there was a cold, rainy drizzle. This made no difference to us, of course. Each of us knew precisely where the moon was situated. We could feel its pull from behind the clouds.

We no longer felt tired. All of us felt immensely exhilarated by our return to earth. We also knew instinctively that there would now be no difficulty in stopping this war. Whether the parasites could be defeated or not was another matter.

Our practice in space had served us well. With the earth braced against us, it seemed the easiest thing in the world to lock our minds in parallel. This time, there was no need for

Reich, Fleishman and me to act as controllers; the worst that could happen now was that we might shake down the White House.

There was immense exhilaration as our minds combined, such a sense of power as I have never known before. All at once, I knew what is meant by the phrase: we are ' members of one another ', but in a deeper, realler sense than before. I had a vision of the whole human race in constant telepathic contact, and able to combine their psychic powers in this manner. Man as a ' human ' being would cease to exist; the vistas of power would be infinite.

Our wills locked like a great searchlight beam, and stabbed out at the moon. At this stage, we made no effort to increase the power through vibration. The actual contact with the moon was a surprise. It was suddenly as if we were in the middle of the noisiest crowd the world has ever known. The disturbing vibrations from the moon were transmitted directly along the taut cable of force that stretched between us. In fact, there was no audible noise; but for a few seconds our minds lost contact as the tidal wave of psychic disturbance broke over us. Then we combined again and braced ourselves against it. The beam of will grasped the moon, felt its shape, as a hand might feel an orange. For a moment, we gripped gently, waiting. Then, guided by Reich and myself, we began to generate pure motive power. The moon's distance seemed to make no difference. From this, I inferred that our strength was so great that a mere quarter of a million miles was a stone's throw. In the next twenty minutes we put this to the test. It was important to do it slowly, not to waste our strength. This giant, five thousand billion ton globe, was swinging gently on the end of the thread of earth's gravity, unable to escape. In a sense, therefore, it was weightless: all its weight was supported by the earth.

And slowly, very slowly, we exerted a gentle pressure at the moon's surface, a pressure designed to make it rotate. At first, nothing happened. We increased the force, braced tightly against the earth. (Most of us found it more convenient to sit down, in spite of the wet.) Still nothing happened. We were holding it gently, completely untired, and allowing the force waves to build up almost of their own accord. At the end of a quarter of an hour, we knew we had succeeded. The moon was moving, but very, very slowly. We were like children pushing a giant roundabout. Once the initial inertia had been overcome, there was no limit to the speed we could induce by gently increasing the pressure.

But the roundabout was not rotating in a direction parallel to the earth. Instead, we made it rotate at right angles to its own line of motion around the earth – that is to say, in a North-South direction.

The North-South circumference of the moon is roughly six thousand miles long. We continued to apply the force until the point of its application was moving at three thousand miles an hour. This took a little over five minutes, after we had overcome its inertial mass. This meant that the moon would rotate on its own axis once every two hours – a speed that should serve our purpose in every way.

We went indoors again and drank hot coffee. Fifteen leading senators had joined us by now, and the room was overcrowded. We asked them to be quiet, and then all sat there, our minds focused on the moon, to see whether our manoeuvre had worked.

It had. Within twenty minutes, a half of the segment that our moon usually presents to the earth was turned away from us, into outer space. A half of the face that this earth has never seen was turned towards us. And, just as we surmised, the moon's disturbing forces were halved. For thousands of years, these beams of psychic energy had been directed towards the earth. Now they were pointing away into space. The frozen vital forces in the moon no longer had active intelligence. They were not able to assess the situation and recognize that their home was rotating. Besides, it was rotating in a manner that complicated the situation. For centuries, their attention had been directed at the earth, which rotates from left to right, with a surface velocity of a little over a thousand miles an hour. Now their own home was rotating at right angles to the earth. The result was inevitably confusion.

At the end of an hour, the former dark side of the moon was turned entirely towards the earth. The disturbing vibrations from the moon had almost ceased. We asked various senators if they noticed any difference. Some did not; others looked slightly puzzled, and said that it felt more ' peaceful ' than an hour ago.

It was then we were able to tell the President what he had to say. The plan was simple and obvious enough. He had only to declare that an American space research station on the moon had been wiped out, after reporting the presence of gigantic aliens, who had arrived in force.

He seemed sceptical about whether it would work. We assured him it would, and sent him to get some sleep.

I was not present when the President made his historic broadcast. I was taking my longest and deepest sleep since we left earth a fortnight before. I left orders that no one was to awake me. So when I woke up at ten o'clock, it was to learn that our first result had been achieved. The whole world had been tuned in to the President's television appearance. In the larger cities of the world, the news of the moon's axial rotation had already caused hysterical excitement. (And I had reason to reproach myself, for my old friend Sir George Gibbs, the Astronomer Royal, had collapsed with a heart attack when he saw it through the telescope of Greenwich observatory; he died a few hours later.) The President's announcement of aliens on the moon verified everyone's worst fears. No one asked why aliens should have caused the moon to rotate. But that it *was* rotating was plainly visible to every eye during the next twenty-four hours. It was almost at the full. Over large areas of Asia and Europe visibility was perfect. Admittedly, the rotation was not immediately visible – any more than the movement of a clock's minute hand is visible – but anyone who stared at it for more than ten minutes could see plainly that its major landmarks were moving slowly from North to South.

We had hoped that this news would turn everyone's thoughts away from war, but we had reckoned without the parasites. At midday, we heard that six hydrogen rockets had been fired into northern Yugoslavia and Italy, destroying an area of over a thousand square miles. Hazard was determined not to end the war without firing a shot. It would have been convenient if he had at least killed Gwambe. But apparently he hadn't – Gwambe made a television appearance later that afternoon, and swore that, aliens or no aliens, he would never forgive Hazard for this slaughter of his men. (Actually, it was mainly Italian and Yugoslav civilians who died; the bulk of Gwambe's forces were further south.) From now on, Gwambe said, it was total warfare to destroy the white races.

At six o'clock that evening, the news was better. Thousands of Gwambe's men were deserting. The prospect of alien invasion from the moon made them anxious to be with their own families. But still Gwambe announced that his men would fight to the death. A few hours later, the town of Graz in Styria was destroyed by a hydrogen rocket. Half a million of Hazard's men died. Three more rockets landed in open country between Graz and Klagenfurt, killing only a few people but devastating hundreds of square miles. Late that night, we heard that Hazard's forces had finally crossed the border into Yugoslavia and had engaged a large force of Gwambe's men at Maribor. The actual town of Maribor had been completely destroyed by the cosmic ray gun, and the clash of armies took place a mile outside the town.

Now suddenly it was clear that we had to act. We had hoped that this moon-threat would stop the war for a few days, and give the World Security Council time to act. What had the parasites to gain by continuing the war? If the world

205

was destroyed – as it undoubtedly would be – they would be destroyed, too. On the other hand, if the war could be stopped, their chances of survival were almost non-existent. Now we knew the secret – that the parasites lost their nerve in outer space – we could destroy thousands of them a day (unless, of course, they learned to adapt to this new threat). Perhaps they hoped that a few thousand people would survive the cataclysm, as they had survived earlier moon-disasters. Whatever the reason, it looked as if they were determined that the human race should commit suicide.

The important thing was haste. If Gwambe or Hazard was really out for universal destruction, it would not be too difficult. Even a fairly incompetent engineer could easily convert a ' clean ' H bomb into a cobalt bomb with a jacket of cobalt; it could be done in twenty-four hours. It is true that even in this event, the human race could still be saved; it would simply be a matter of finding some way of clearing the atmosphere of cobalt sixty. Our psychokinetic powers were capable of dealing with the problem, but it could take months or years. Perhaps the parasites reckoned on this.

In Durango, Colorado, a group of scientists had been working on a type of space rocket powered by giant photon sails. We had heard talk about it at Base 91. It was constructed of a specially light alloy of lithium and beryllium, and was enormous in size – as it had to be to support its giant sails.

I spoke to the President. How far had the project advanced? Could the ship be used yet? He contacted the Durango base and came back with the answer: No. The structure was complete, but the engines were still in the experimental stage.

I told the President this was unimportant. All we needed was the ship. And it had to be sprayed black. The base replied this was impossible: its surface area was nearly two square miles. The President scowled and shouted into the telescreen. Then he pulled out the plug. He told me that the ship would be black by the time a rocket plane could get us to Durango.

The sheer size of the ship startled us. It was being constructed in the immense crater made by the impact of the 1980 meteor. Its construction was top secret. The crater was roofed with an opaque force barrier. And under this barrier the Durango rocket looked like an immense and foreshortened bullet. Its largest flat area was its rear end, which housed the sails. This was two thousand feet high.

We arrived at the Durango base five hours after the President's call. The whole place stank of cellulose paint, and everything was covered with black spray. The men themselves were all black from head to foot. But the ship itself was also black, every inch of it.

It was nearly midnight. We told Major-General Gates, the station commander, that all the men were to be sent home, and the force barrier was to be withdrawn. He had been told to obey every order without question, and he gave us excellent co-operation. But I have never seen a man look so completely puzzled.

He showed us the mechanism for operating the photon sails. These had not been painted black, and they were of bright silver, and shaped roughly like a butterfly's wings.

I must admit that we all felt a little absurd, standing in the immense silver hall. It was icy cold and smelt of spray paint. The controls had been installed, but very little else. There was another year's work to be done on the interior. There were only six seats at the front, near the controls. The others had to sit on camp stools that had been installed for them.

But as soon as we began the work of getting it off the ground, this feeling of absurdity vanished. There were no difficulties; the shell was extremely light. One man could have moved it alone. As it was, we assigned the task of powering the ship to a ten man team led by Ebner. I undertook the steering. The only man who was not a member of our team was Captain Haydon Reynolds of the U.S. Air

Force, the navigator. He obviously wondered what he was doing there, since a ship without engines needs no navigator.

We lifted off at twenty minutes after midnight, rose to a height of ten thousand feet, and proceeded due east. Reynolds was so astounded for the first quarter of an hour that it was difficult to get any coherent instructions from him. Then he settled down, and from then on the flight was uneventful.

The American defence system had been warned that we would be breaking through the early warning system at half past midnight, and we had no trouble. At a quarter to one, our television set brought warning that some immense intruder had entered the earth's atmosphere from the direction of the moon. This was according to the instructions we had left with the President.

Over the Atlantic, we accelerated to a speed of a thousand miles an hour. The result was that the temperature in the ship increased uncomfortably. But time was important. When we set out from Durango, it would already be half past eight in the morning at Maribor. We had five thousand miles to travel, and it was important to do it before evening fell.

Before we crossed the European coast, we increased height to twenty five thousand feet. We knew that early warning systems all over France and England would be ringing by this time, and that we would need constant vigilance.

The first rocket was launched at us from somewhere near Bordeaux. Ten of our team under Reich were maintaining the force barrier around the ship, and exploded it when it was two miles away from us. Unfortunately, Reich forgot to block the force waves, with the result that we were all suddenly tossed about like corks in a storm. For a few seconds we lost control, then I managed to block the force waves, and we moved forward smoothly again. After that, Reich took care to direct the force of the explosion away from us.

The television screens showed us that our passage was universally observed. The explosion of the missiles that were aimed at us left no one in any doubt that we were the moon-aliens, and that we had some kind of destructive ray.

By one o'clock, European time, we were directly over the battlefield at Maribor. We had reduced height to a few thousand feet. Since our method of propulsion made no sound, we could distinctly hear the explosion of shells underneath us.

It was as well that we had chosen a ship of this size. The battlefield was enormous – ten miles across. There were no large troop concentrations – only the small groups of men who handled the mobile guns and rocket launchers. Our size meant that we could be plainly seen by both sides, even though the ground was covered with a thick haze of smoke.

Now began the major part of the operation – and the part whose success we were unable to guarantee. It would have been easy enough to destroy all life within that area of a hundred square miles, and put a complete stop to the fighting. And yet none of us would have been able to do this. We had nothing but contempt for the men who were trying to kill one another, but we felt we had no right to kill them.

The first thing was to immobilize the mobile rocket units. Within ten minutes of our appearance, a dozen of them had tried firing rockets at us. The missiles were destroyed, and Reich's group then destroyed each of the launching machines by simply crushing them out of shape. But there were probably a thousand or so large guns and rocket launchers on the battlefield; we had to make sure of each of these, too. We wanted to be able to concentrate fully on the major part of the task. It took us nearly an hour of groping around in the smoke to locate every gun and launching site, and to destroy it.

Our first appearance had caused a panic. But when no death-rays came from us, it subsided. The operation of immobilizing the guns was unspectacular; only those in actual contact with them noticed it. So after a while, everyone regarded us with curiosity rather than fear. Our mental 'feelers' were aware of this, and we actively encouraged the mood.

It was a strange feeling. We all sat there, in complete silence. The only sound was the wind. All firing from below us had stopped. We were aware of being watched by a million men massed in two great armies. I was even aware of the presence of the parasites in many of them, for the response that came from the ' zombis ' was cold and incurious, unlike the human response.

At this point, Fleishman touched the button that controlled the photon sails, and they slowly opened. It must have been an impressive sight – these immense silver wings that first of all slid out of the back of the ship, then slowly expanded until they were four times bigger than the ship, with a total area of eight square miles. We now looked like a giant insect with a black body, and shiny but almost transparent wings.

It must be understood that we were in close contact with our ' audience ', as close and intimate as any such contact between an actor and his audience in a theatre. Consequently we were able to register the reaction of astonishment that contained only an element of fear.

As we began to move very slowly across the sky, I became aware of a change in the quality of the response. They were watching this great silver object with fascination, but no longer with intelligent curiosity. Their active attention was flagging – which is hardly surprising, since no one had taken their eyes off us for over an hour. The sunlight on the photon sails was dazzling.

For them, we looked like a gigantic and beautiful insect, too bright to watch with comfort, and yet too fascinating to lose sight of.

The effect was exactly what we had supposed. The quality of the attention became flaccid and hypnotic as we moved very slowly, drifting across the sky, gradually dropping towards the ground. This slow, gentle movement was a considerable effort for Reich's team, since the huge wing area meant that the ship was being constantly buffeted by wind, which would have sent it spinning if their vigilance relaxed for a moment.

The other forty of us now linked in parallel. These watching minds were completely in our power, like a child fascinated by a story. I also observed an interesting thing that I had always suspected: all of these spectators were also telepathically linked together by their interest in us. It explains why mobs can be so dangerous. An excited crowd builds up a certain telepathic force by a vibratory process, but in a clumsy and unco-ordinated manner, so that it feels impelled to violent action to release the tension.

The tension of this crowd was at our disposal. It was like one enormous mind opened to us. This mind was wholly concentrated on a great, insect-like object, that was now very close to the ground. They were hypnotized and completely open to suggestion.

The central part of the operation was now in my hands. Their minds were like so many television screens, and I was the central transmitter. The consequence was that every one of them suddenly became aware that two huge doors were opening in the sides of the space ship. And then from these doors – more than a thousand feet high – stepped the moon aliens. The aliens were also more than a thousand feet high. They were also suggestive of insects, being green in colour, and possessed of long legs like a grasshopper. Their faces were humanoid, with great beaky noses, and small black eyes. They moved in a jerky way, as if unused to the earth's gravity. Their feet were claws, like a bird's.

Then, in great leaps, the aliens moved across the ground towards the watching armies. I transmitted nightmare waves of panic, certainty of a horrible destruction. At the same time, I released the tension that held them all to the spot, watching helplessly. The result was a stampede away from

211

us. The sense of panic was so unpleasant – almost indecent in its abject terror – that we broke telepathic contact with them, and left them to run. No one looked back. Thousands fell and were trampled to death; later figures showed that fifteen per cent of them died in this way. The havoc could hardly have been increased even if the hostile aliens had been real.

It was a highly unpleasant experience. For weeks afterwards, I kept remembering that panic; it returned like a bad taste in the mouth. But it was necessary. It certainly ended the war. From that moment on, Gwambe and Hazard were no longer leaders. They were ignored, forgotten. The war was a dream from which everybody had awakened, a children's game that had come to an end. Over the next three days, troops of the World Organization, acting in close co-operation with the President of the United States, were able to arrest thousands of the scattered armies, including Gwambe and Hazard. (The latter was shot while ' attempting to escape '; Gwambe was confined in a lunatic asylum in Geneva, where he died a year later.)

It might be assumed that after this victory, we felt inclined to rest on our laurels. In fact, we felt nothing of the sort, for two reasons. The victory had been child's play. I have related it in some detail here because of its historical interest, but as a piece of strategy it barely deserves two lines. Second, the really interesting part of our task now lay ahead of us: to restore the world to some kind of sanity, and to consider measures for the final destruction of the parasites.

There was nothing spectacular in the methods we adopted. We simply told people the truth. On the day after our ' victory ', President Melville announced on television that the United States government had every reason to believe that the ' moon aliens ' were on their way out of our solar system, and that there was no longer any immediate danger to our

212

planet. He added: 'But in view of the constant danger of an extra-terrestrial attack, the United States urges the immediate formation of a Unified World Government, armed with full powers for mobilizing a World Defence Force.' His proposal was immediately accepted by the United Nations. And then began the great task which has been so ably documented by Wolfgang Reich in his book *The Remaking of the World.*

Our most serious task, of course, was the destruction of the parasites. But we decided that this was not an immediate priority. The rotation of the moon had the effect of considerably diminishing their power by lessening the basic source of irritation. But there was another reason for treating them as a secondary problem. I have said that, in a sense, the parasites were a 'shadow' of man's cowardice and passivity. Their strength could increase in an atmosphere of defeat and panic, for it fed on human fear. In that case, the best way to combat them was to change the atmosphere to one of strength and purpose. And this we regarded as our major task during the next year. The first problem was to make the World Security Force really effective, to stamp out any sign of renewed activity on the part of the parasites. This meant that about twenty of our group had to apply themselves to problems of organization. Almost equally important was to make people understand that the parasites were a reality, against which mankind had to maintain constant vigilance. And this in turn meant that we had to increase our group until it could be numbered in thousands, or even millions. For this reason only twenty of us (including Ebner and Fleishman) were assigned to the World Security Organization. The rest of us applied ourselves to the task of teaching.

I must say a few words about this since, in fact, everything depended upon our success in this field. It was by no means an easy matter to pick candidates to be taught the techniques of 'mind control'. It might seem that there was no problem at all; after all, I had taught myself; so had Reich and Fleishman. Surely we only had to announce the facts about the mind parasites to the human race, and men would teach themselves?

This is only partly true. It happened, certainly. But this in itself raised a problem. The battle against the mind parasites requires a peculiarly tough and active intelligence; most people are so mentally lazy that they can easily be out-manoeuvred by the parasites. They are now in a dangerous position, for they have a sense of false security, which the parasites are careful to foster. Here is certainly a case where a little knowledge is dangerous.

But the fact that about three-quarters of the human race immediately came to believe that they had achieved perfect ' mind control ' set us a great problem. How were we to know which of these millions was worth our personal attention? It was not a problem we managed to solve immediately. We worked by hit and miss methods. We confined ourselves to highly intelligent people, particularly those who had ' worked their way up,' since our most important requirement was courage and vitality. But there were a great many failures. When Reich and I had achieved our initial victories over the parasites, we had been stimulated by a sense of immediate danger. These new candidates were not, and many of them simply could not wake themselves up to a sense of urgency. I came to realize how much of ' success ' in the world is due to a mere habit of aggressiveness and hard work, and not at all to intelligence. We had no time to waste on the failures. If we had used our telepathic powers to ' wake them up ', it would only have increased their laziness. So they were quickly dismissed, and others admitted in their place.

It soon struck us that even quite intelligent and serious people could suffer from mental laziness if they had acquired the habit in childhood. So we decided that our future candidates would have to be caught as early as possible. For this reason, a number of us formed a separate group for testing the mental capacities of teenagers and children. This became the so-called ' Behrman K-Test Group ' whose success

214

exceeded all our expectations – within two years there were more than five hundred thousand mind control 'adepts' under the age of 21.

At the end of a year, we knew we had won our battle to establish permanent world peace. We could now turn our attention back to the moon. This was by now necessary. The disturbing forces of the moon had become accustomed to its unusual motion, and were re-focused on the earth. This was exactly what I had expected to happen; the rotation of the moon was only a temporary measure.

Without consulting anyone about it, a group of five hundred of us decided that the moon would have to be detached from earth's gravitational field. We commenced work on this operation in January 1999 – the last New Year's Day of the old century. It was largely an engineering problem. It meant exerting a constant pressure on the moon for a very long period, and never relaxing this pressure. The operation had to be carried out very slowly. The moon's density is very low compared with that of the earth; it is little more than an enormous cinder. In its long life it has also been struck by innumerable meteors and comets, some of them very large indeed, so that it had been flawed through and through. like a lump of cracked glass. This meant that there was danger of its flying apart if we exerted any sudden pressure; in which case, the earth would become surrounded by a ring of lunar asteroids, and we would be no better off.

Our intention was not simply to shield earth from the moon's emanations. There was also the desire to do something about the life trapped in the satellite. We decided that the moon must be pushed into the sun, where its bodiless inhabitants might once again be free.

Four groups of a hundred and twenty-five of us spaced ourselves out in the northern hemisphere, and commenced the work of pushing the moon gently into outer space. What this meant in effect was increasing its speed of revolution around the earth, imparting to it more energy. This in turn would mean that the moon would move further from the earth.

(The moon was once much farther from the earth than it was in the twentieth century, but as it lost energy it tended to fall closer.)

Over the course of the year 1999, we increased the moon's speed of revolution from 28 days to 14. This was not a difficult task; by this time, I already knew enough about the secrets of the mind and its relation to the material universe to have been capable of doing it alone. It was now a million miles away from the earth, which meant that its speed of orbit had been multiplied by ten. We calculated that this speed would have to be doubled (to forty thousand miles an hour) before the moon would ' escape '. It would then be drawn automatically towards the sun. This finally happened on February 22nd of the year 2,000. The earth lost its moon, to the accompaniment of violent protests from sentimentalists, which we ignored. We had made one slight miscalculation; three months later, when crossing the orbit of Mercury, the moon was caught in the planet's gravitational field. But since the mass of Mercury is approximately the same as that of the moon, there was no question of the moon becoming its satellite. Mercury was pulled seven million miles closer to the sun; the moon finally fell into orbit around the sun at an average distance of nineteen million miles. At this distance, the surface temperature is high enough to keep the rocks in a perpetually molten state. The moon's ' life ' has at least been granted a certain degree of freedom.

There is a point at which I have to stop; not because there is no more to say, but because what remains to be said is too difficult to express in this context.

To the average human being of today, it must seem that we ' initiates ' have achieved the status of gods. In a sense, we have – compared with the human beings of the twentieth century. In another sense, we are as far from that goal as

216

ever. We are no longer limited by ignorance and lack of purpose; but our ignorance is still enormous. The road we have to travel still stretches into the distance. It is impossible for me to explain the nature of the problems that confront us. If human beings were capable of understanding, there would be no need to explain.

I do not know whether to regard myself as fortunate or unfortunate. I am fortunate in having been the spearhead of this great movement in human evolution. I now understand what remains to be done. I am unfortunate in the sense of having lost contact with the rest of the human race – with a few important exceptions. Man is lazy by nature, and laziness is by no means to be condemned. It means he dislikes inconvenience, and he has created civilization to escape inconvenience; so his laziness has been an important factor in his evolution. But this also means that he prefers to evolve at his own slow and deliberate rate. The battle against the mind parasites has geared me to a faster rate of evolution; it has made me impatient to move on. I cannot be contented to know that the endless realms of mind now lie open for man's exploration; this does not seem enough. There are too many questions unanswered. It is true that man can no longer be separated from his sense of evolutionary purpose, and it now seems likely that men will live for centuries instead of dying out of boredom and defeat at the age of eighty. But we still do not know what happens when a man dies, or when existence is created from non-existence. We know there is a benevolent principle of purpose in the universe, but we still do not know whether this principle is the ultimate Creator of the Bible, or whether it depends upon some still deeper source. The mystery of time remains untouched; so does the fundamental question asked by Heidegger: Why is there existence rather than non-existence? The answer may lie in a completely different dimension, as different from the world of mind as mind is different from the world of space and time . . .

(We have chosen to conclude the account at this point, with a section from Austin's unpublished journals, because it seems to the editor that these passages offer a possible solution to the mystery of the *Pallas*. So many words have been devoted to this ' *Marie Celeste* of space ' that the facts have tended to become blurred. The following extract from Captain James Ramsay's *Autobiography* sets out the known facts clearly:

In January of the year 2007, the government of the United States announced that it had placed its space vehicle *Pallas*, the largest space craft yet built, at the disposal of an expedition that was to be led by Professors Reich and Austin. Their announced purpose was an archaeological expedition to the planet Pluto, in the hope of uncovering traces of vanished civilizations. Two days before the expedition's departure, an article by Horace Kimmell in *World Press News* stated that the true purpose of the expedition was to discover whether Pluto could be the base of the immense space ships that had been reported in the upper atmosphere . . . This was categorically denied by Professor Austin.

The *Pallas*, with a crew of 2,000, all carefully chosen by the leaders of the expedition (and including, incidentally, all but seven members of the earlier expedition of 1997), set out from Washington on February 2nd, 2007, and was last contacted shortly before midnight on that day, when Professor Austin's voice announced that the ship had covered about a million miles. After this, all attempts to establish contact with the *Pallas* failed . . .

Exactly ten years later, on February 10, 2017, an expedition headed by myself set out with the specific purpose of discovering traces of the *Pallas*. There were three space craft, the *Centaur*, the *Clio* and the *Leicester*. Pluto was reached on January 12th, 2018. A month later, after four circuits of the planet, we prepared to return to earth. It was then that the *Clio* picked up the distinctive radio signals of the *Pallas* . . .
It was finally located on March 2, 2018, floating about two million miles from Pluto. The lights of this enormous ship

were all burning, and its freedom from external damage gave us reason to hope that some of its crew might have survived. However, when there was no response to signals. I agreed that this was unlikely, and ordered Lieutenant Firmin to cut through the ship's emergency lock. A party led by myself then entered the *Pallas*, and found it completely deserted. There was no sign of violence, and the condition of the personal belongings of the crew seemed to indicate that they had not expected to evacuate the ship. The log of the *Pallas* had been filled in up to June 9, 2007, and showed that the ship had spent some time on Pluto, and intended to make its way to Neptune when Pluto's perihelion corresponded to Neptune's aphelion. The ship's automatic recording instruments had continued to function normally since that date, but indicated that the *Pallas* had been floating freely in space. There was no indication that the ship had been approached by any foreign body larger than a fifty pound meteor, which had been automatically repelled. They also indicated that the doors of the *Pallas* had not been opened since it left Pluto. A theory put forward by the *Clio*'s chief physician, to the effect that the crew of the *Pallas* had been spontaneously atomized by some exploding source of cosmic rays that would affect only organic matter, was disproved by the evidence of a Dunbar Assimilator.

The engines of the *Pallas* had been switched off normally at 9.30 p.m. on June 9th, and the ship had been brought to a halt. The engines still proved to be in perfect working condition when tested by us.

The *Pallas* was brought back to earth, piloted by Lieutenant Firmin, and arrived on December 10, 2018. Subsequent investigations did nothing to clear up the mystery, and later expeditions to Pluto and Neptune failed to produce new evidence.

The view of the present editor, as I have made clear elsewhere, is that the disappearance of the *Pallas* was planned, and that when the space craft set out from earth in February 2007 every man aboard knew that he would never return. No other theory fits the facts. There is no evidence whatever that the *Pallas* was the victim of a surprise attack, and that its instruments were somehow re-set to destroy the evidence. Neither is there any evidence to indicate that the crew of the *Pallas* intended to build a new civilization on another planet. There were only three women on board. The number would surely have been higher if any such plan had been contemplated?

In my own view, the present edition of *The Mind Parasites* offers definite clues about what became of the *Pallas*. The passage on page 271 and 272 dealing with the 'universal police', drawn from Austin's unpublished papers, seems to us the most important of these. He says: 'The nearest of these receivers was situated only about four thousand million miles away, a cruising ship from a planet in the Proxima Centauri system'. In November 1997, at the time this refers to, Pluto was almost at its aphelion distance from the sun (4,567 million miles). It is possible therefore that the 'receiver' Austin speaks of was somewhere near Pluto – although of course, it could have been in any other direction. Could the 'universal police' from Proxima Centauri have had some sort of a base on Pluto? Again, where did Kimmel gain access to the information that the real purpose of the expedition was to see whether Pluto could be the base of the saucer-like space ships that had been seen by so many people in the early years of this century? Kimmel died in a rocket plane accident two months after the *Pallas* set out for Pluto, and never revealed the source of the rumour. But he was known as an honest and level-headed journalist who stuck close to the facts. It seems unlikely that he simply invented the story.

Finally, we have Austin's own words, written only a month before that final expedition, stating that he had 'lost contact with the rest of the human race', and that the battle against the parasites had 'geared him to a faster rate of evolution'. In the light of the passage about the 'universal police', could anything be more natural than that Austin should plan to leave earth and join them?

But above all, what could be stranger than the brevity of Austin's reference to the 'space police'? This is surely a matter on which one might have expected him to spend several pages? Some clue as to his reason for this silence is given in a manuscript of Dagobert Ferris, another member of that original expedition, and author of *Towards a Psychology of the Golden Age*. Ferris also vanished on the *Pallas*, but he left behind an account of a conversation that took place between himself and Professor Reich after they had become aware of the existence of these 'space police'. In part, it runs as follows:

'We speculated about the appearance of these Beings. Were they the same as ourselves, with arms and legs? Or would they resemble some strange animal or fish – perhaps an octopus? Would they simply take over the government of the earth and restore peace, or would they take stern repressive measures against people like Hazard and Gwambe?'

[This passage in itself is strange enough. Why should he assume that the 'police' would be taking over the earth? Had Austin actually *spoken to them* about this possibility? And had it been finally decided that Austin and his associates could handle the Gwambe crisis?]

'I felt happy at this prospect of a new " government " for the earth. Ever since the " death of God " in the eighteenth century, man has had a feeling of being alone in an empty universe, the feeling that it is no use looking to the heavens for guidance. He is like a child who has wakened up one morning to be told that his father is dead and that he must now take over the position as head of the family. This feeling of fatherlessness is surely one of the greatest psychological shocks that anyone can suffer? We can all remember that feeling we had at school, where hard work brought immediate rewards, prizes at the end of term, praise from the headmaster, favours from the prefects. Then you leave school and there is no one " above " you any more. You are out on your own. (I must admit that I was tempted to join the army when

I left school, merely to have that feeling of " belonging " to a group again.) And you get a strange feeling of emptiness, of the meaninglessness of anything you do. Surely this is what lies behind the " moral bankruptcy " of the twentieth century?

'And now all this was over. There *were* greater powers than man, powers that we could look up to. Life would be really meaningful again, the emptiness would be filled . . . The human race could go back to school. And why not, since it was largely composed of schoolboys?

'Reich disagreed with me. He asked: " Don't you think that's *our* job?" I said: " No, I'd rather learn than teach ". At this point, Austin interrupted with the remark: " I agree with Reich. Nothing could be more dangerous for the human race than to believe that its affairs had fallen into the hands of supermen ".'

For my own part, I believe that this is the reason why Austin refused help from the ' space police '. I believe it is also the reason why he decided that a time had come when he himself should vanish – vanish in such a way that the human race could never be certain of his death.

And since it seems certain that no further evidence will ever be forthcoming, we have no alternative than to keep an open mind on the subject.